Name _____

Color words rhyming with **cat** red.

Color all other words yellow.

The mystery letter is _____

wag	rat	pat	hat	tap
fan	bat	man	sad	wax
cab	sat	fat	bag	sap
tan	mat	ham	ran	cap
sad	slat	bag	map	pan

FS-32031 Reading Activities

Name _____

Color all words rhyming with **took** | **blue** .

Color all other words | **yellow** .

The mystery number is [   ]

fog	book	mop	hook	sock
top	cook	pot	book	mop
roof	hook	look	hook	book
moon	dock	lock	cook	pop
boot	cool	log	look	mob

2

Name _____

Color words rhyming with **bed** blue.

Color all other words yellow.

The mystery letter is [   ]

wept	Ted	get	creep	he
bet	fed	me	we	wet
set	led	fret	met	slept
weed	red	seed	need	deed
let	Fred	sled	shed	Ned

FS-32031 Reading Activities

Name _____

Color words rhyming with **hay** red.

Color all other words **yellow**.

The mystery word is [   ]

may	boy	pry	way	rat
joy	toy	pay	say	day
tray	fry	cat	lay	try
gray	fly	lad	bay	cry
stay	my	hat	ray	mad

FS-32031 Reading Activities

Name _____

Start with | **rate**. |

1. Don't be _____ .
2. Close the _____ .
3. Eat a_____ .
4. To **not** like: _____

| hate |
| late |
| date |
| gate |

_____

Start with | **pain**. |

1. A spot: _____
2. To add weight: _____
3. From the clouds: _____
4. Choo, choo _____

| train |
| rain |
| stain |
| gain |

_____

Start with | **ray**. |

1. Know your _____ .
2. Monday is a _____ .
3. Black and white make _____ .
4. To put down: _____

| lay |
| gray |
| day |
| way |

Name _____

Start with | **crime.**

1. The bells _____ .
2. Two nickels: _____
3. Clock: _____
4. A green fruit: _____

dime
lime
chime
time

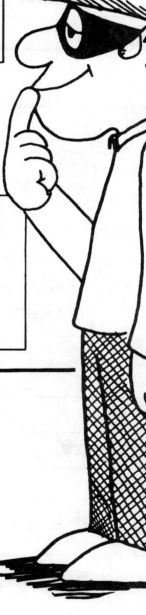

Start with | **gripe.**

1. A zebra has a _____ .
2. Smoke a _____ .
3. Clean off: _____
4. Ready to eat: _____

pipe
ripe
stripe
wipe

Start with | **mine.**

1. A number: _____
2. Draw a _____ .
3. I feel _____ .
4. A tree: _____

fine
nine
pine
line

Name _____

If it rhymes with **man**, color it **red**.
If it rhymes with **noon**, color it **yellow**.
If it rhymes with **rock**, color it **green**.
If it rhymes with **float**, color it **blue**.

   FS-32031 Reading Activities

If it rhymes with **mail**, put a **red dot** on it.

If it rhymes with **bar**, mark it with **green**.

If it rhymes with **see**, make a **yellow X** on it.

If it rhymes with **ring**, color it **red**.
If it rhymes with **big**, color it **yellow**.
If it rhymes with **wet**, color it **blue**.
If it rhymes with **Ben**, color it **green**.

Directions: Paste a [boat] to [sail].
Make a new word.
Write the compound word.

[sail] [boat]

sailboat

rattle

base

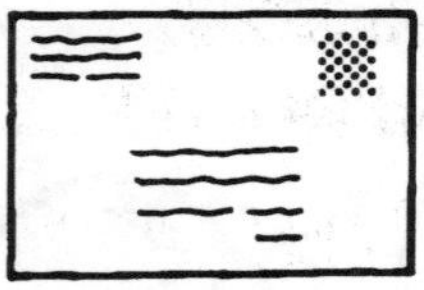

mail

pan

flag

_____

_____

_____

_____

_____

ball    cakes    snake    pole    man

FS-32031 Reading Activities

Name _____

Directions: Make a compound word from 2 words.
Write the word.

1.  flag + pole

_____

2. base + ball

_____

3. dog + house

_____

4. butter + fly

_____

5. hair + brush

_____

6. lady + bug

_____

7. bare + foot

_____

8. shoe + lace

_____

9. play + pen

_____

10. cup + cake

_____

FS-32031 Reading Activities

Name ______________________ Skill: Compound Words

Directions: Write the two words that make up each compound word.

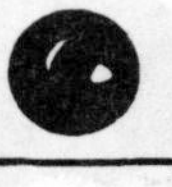

 blueberry

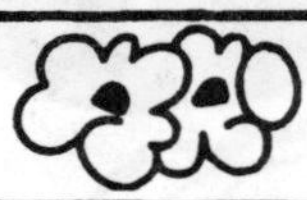

 popcorn

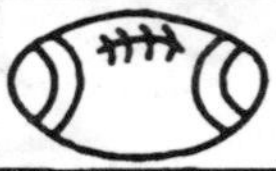

 football

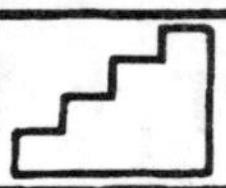

 downstairs

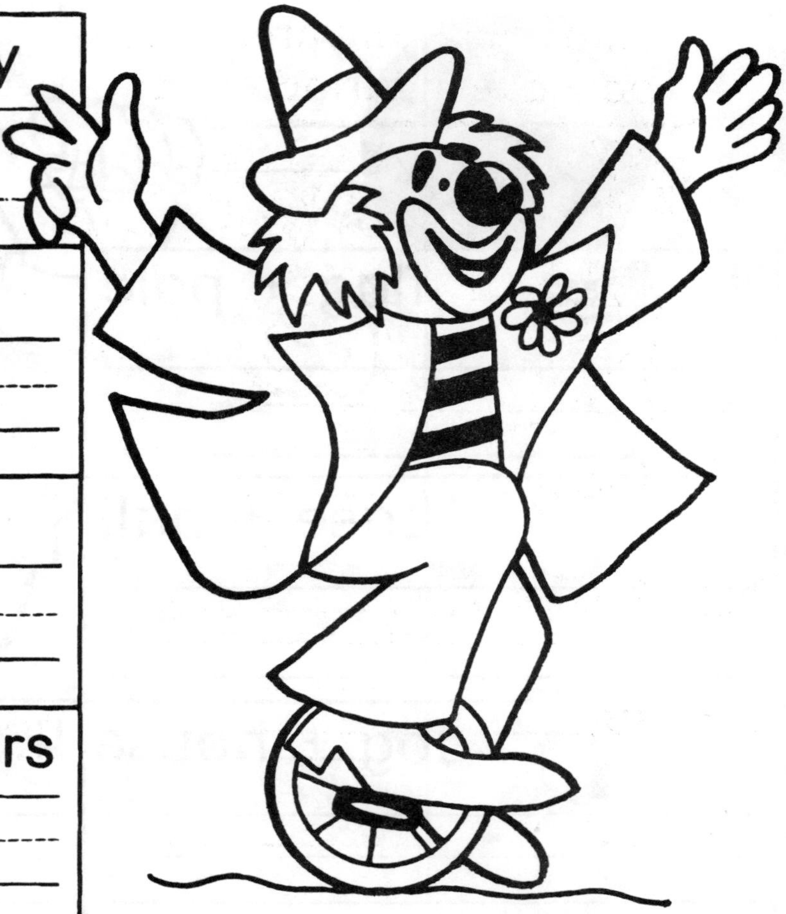

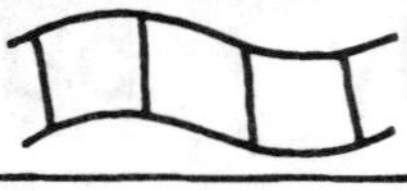

 sidewalk

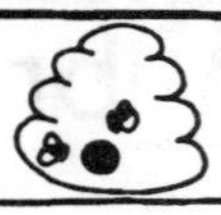

 beehive

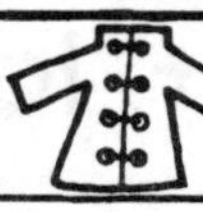

 raincoat

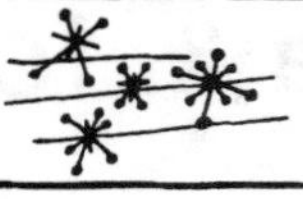

 snowstorm

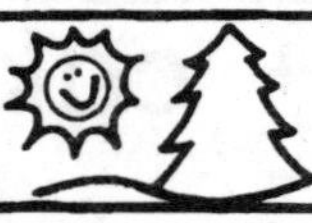

 outside

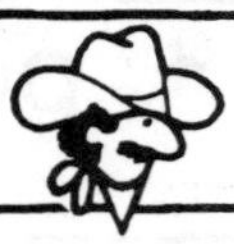

 cowboy

Directions: Write the missing compound word in each sentence.

| sunshine | anyone | fireman | myself | baseball |
| pancakes | birthday | afternoon | doorbell | airplane |

1. Dad is a _____.

2. I ate two_____.

3. Is_____ home?

4. Let's play_____.

5. I saw Kim this_____.

6. The_____ is bright.

7. Today is my_____.

8. I walked home by_____.

9. Let's fly in the_____.

10. Ring the_____.

FS-32031 Reading Activities

Directions: Find a word to go with each meaning.

bookcase	driveway	shoelace	cupboard	doorbell
bathtub	mailbox	bedroom	classroom	doorknob

1. a place for letters _____

2. a place to sleep _____

3. for tying shoes _____

4. a place for books _____

5. for taking a bath _____

6. a place to learn _____

7. use to open door _____

8. place for dishes _____

9. place for the car _____

10. tells you someone is at the door _____

Compound Word Splits

Place the given letters in each grid to form a compound word.
The words go across, then down. Use the pictures below as clues.

Write the completed compound word beside the correct picture.

1. pieo

t		

2. aupke

c		

3. hinnue

s		

4. eciphap

s				

5. htirda

b			

6. ropee

t			

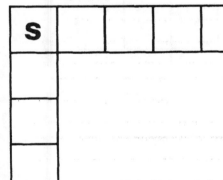
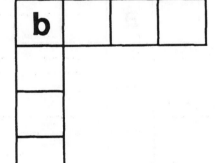
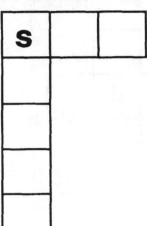

_____   _____   _____

_____   _____   _____

Brainwork! Draw the boxes for compound word splits like the ones above.
Use the words *pinpoint*, *seashell*, and *sunset*.

Compound Word Splits

Place the given letters in each grid to form a compound word.
The words go down, then across. Use the pictures below as clues.

Write the completed compound word beside the correct picture.

1. tcot

u

2. ekpnc

a

3. llshde

i

4. whkrme

o

5. llwtref

a

6. bblsel

a

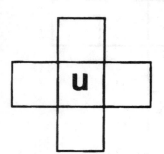

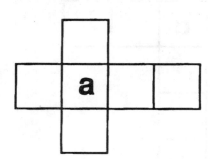

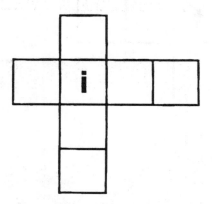

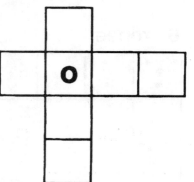

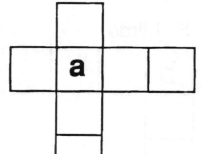

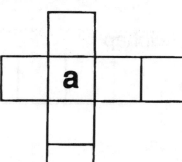

Brainwork! Write a paragraph using the compound words above.

FS-32031 Reading Activities

Directions: Cut and paste [he's] on 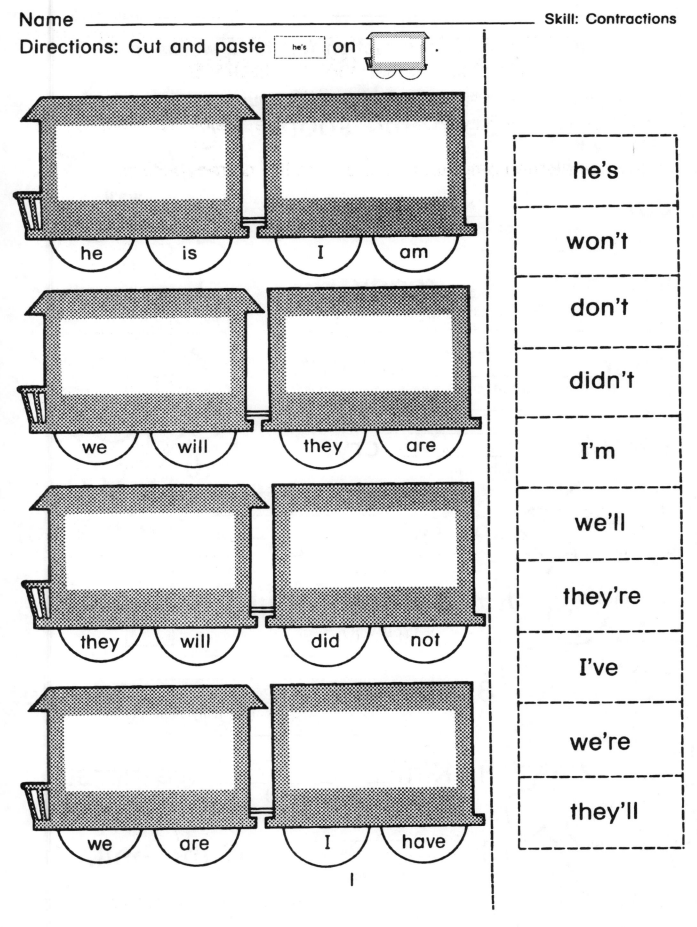 .

he is	I am
we will	they are
they will	did not
we are	I have

he's

won't

don't

didn't

I'm

we'll

they're

I've

we're

they'll

   FS-32031 Reading Activities

Directions: Write a contraction for the 2 words in ( ).

1. _____ be home soon.
(I will)

2. Jan _____ play.
will not

3. We _____ ready.
(are not)

4. That _____ my hat.
(is not)

5. I think _____ cry.
(she will)

she'll

we'll

I'll

they'll

you'll

will

aren't

didn't

isn't

doesn't

won't

6. Tod _____ find the cat.
(did not)

7. _____ like that book.
(You will)

8. Hurry or _____ be late.
(we will)

9. Kim _____ live here.
(does not)

10. _____ ring the bell.
(they will)

Name _____

Directions: Write 2 words from the box for each contraction.

isn't

should not
will not
has not
I have
we have
you have
is not
do not

I've

shouldn't

don't

won't

hasn't

we've

you've

19

Directions: Write 2 words for each contraction.

1. we'll

2. he's   3. I'm   4. didn't

5. aren't   6. they'll   7. won't

8. I'll   9. we're   10. we've

1. _____   2. _____

3. _____   4. _____

5. _____   6. _____

7. _____   8. _____

9. _____   10. _____

Directions: Write contractions. Cross out letters you do not use.

1. we are **we're** _____

2. could not _____

3. he is _____

4. they will _____

5. I am _____

6. we have _____

7. she will _____

8. cannot _____

9. did not _____

10. do not _____

11. she is _____

12. they are _____

FS-32031 Reading Activities

Name _____

Directions: Write a word from the box that has the same meaning.

| pan | yell | house | glue | rip | bag |
| dish | gift | cry | sick | cup | smile |

shout
_____
_____

plate
_____
_____

home
_____
_____

present
_____
_____

grin
_____
_____

weep
_____
_____

paste
_____
_____

tear
_____
_____

ill
_____
_____

mug
_____
_____

pot
_____
_____

sack
_____
_____

Directions: Circle two words that have almost the same meaning.

(large) (big) thin

1. easy   simple   funny

2. tiny   baby   small

3. dance   jump   leap

4. bumpy   rough   heavy

5. hear   look   watch

6. fix   repair   buy

7. stop   start   begin

8. quick   fast   run

9. smile   happy   grin

10. close   shut   open

11. fence   home   house

12. mean   nasty   big

FS-32031 Reading Activities

Directions: Write a word that has almost the same meaning as the underlined word.

like	silly	watch	yell	unhappy
fuzzy	largest	turn	scared	leaped

1. I <u>enjoy</u> watching the clowns. _____

2. The <u>sad</u> clown is the best. _____

3. He is riding the <u>biggest</u> bike. _____

4. Watch the bike <u>spin</u> around. _____

5. Here comes the <u>furry</u> dog. _____

6. He looks <u>funny</u> in a clown's hat. _____

7. Did you <u>see</u> the dog jump? _____

8. It <u>jumped</u> into the basket. _____

9. Is the dog <u>frightened</u>? _____

10. Let's clap and <u>shout</u> for the dog! _____

Take My Place

Choose the word from the Word Box that could take the place of the boldfaced word in each sentence. Write it on the line.

Word Box

| thick | whole | help | choose | careful | piece |

1. I will **select** a new tie for Dad.

_____

4. I'd like a small **portion** of the cake, please.

_____

2. This box is heavy. Will you **assist** me?

_ _ _ _ _ _ _ _ _

5. I didn't see you hiding in those **dense** bushes.

_ _ _ _ _ _ _ _ _

3. Today we saw every animal in the **entire** zoo!

_ _ _ _ _ _ _ _ _

6. Be **cautious** when crossing the street.

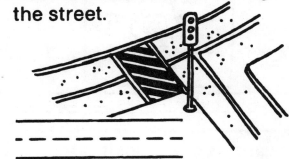

_ _ _ _ _ _ _ _ _

Brainwork! Write five words that could take the place of the word *said*.

Figure It Out

Read each sentence. Use the picture clue to help you figure out the meaning of the boldfaced word. Circle the correct meaning. Write it on the line.

1. The workers are **constructing** a new house on our street.

building   moving

2. Our plane **departed** at ten o'clock.

landed   left

3. I waited for Sandy to **reply**.

answer   visit

4. The teacher corrected my spelling **error**.

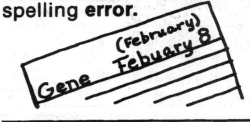

month   mistake

5. Blowing up a balloon **alters** its shape.

changes   colors

6. He will now **demonstrate** how the robot works.

believe   show

Brainwork! List at least five things to which you could *reply*.

Name _____

Directions: Find a word that means the opposite.
Write the number of the antonym.

1. right	2. sun	3. laugh	4. dirty
5. day	6. big	7. sad	8. break
9. full	10. over	11. float	12. open

__2__ moon

____ happy

____ empty

____ clean

____ cry

____ small

____ fix

____ sink

____ left

____ night

____ closed

____ under

FS-32031 Reading Activities

Name _____

Directions: Write an antonym for the word in the ☐ for each sentence.

ugly sink night full bright

heavy wet cold laugh soft

25¢ Balloons

day
1. It is dark at _____.

hard
2. The kitten is _____.

pretty
3. Monsters are _____.

hot
4. Ice cream is _____.

float
5. Wood will not _____.

light
6. The big rock is _____.

dry
7. Snow is cold and _____.

cry
8. Clowns make me _____.

empty
9. The pool is _____.

dark
10. The sun is _____.

Directions: Circle an antonym for the underlined word in each sentence.

Snake Charmer

1. The bike is <u>broken</u>.   (fixed)   old   lost

2. Kim is the <u>tallest</u> girl.   oldest   shortest   cutest

3. That <u>boy</u> is nice.   kid   girl   person

4. Steve is very <u>happy</u>.   angry   funny   sad

5. Can Mark <u>work</u> today?   run   play   eat

6. Jump <u>over</u> the net.   under   beside   on

7. I <u>found</u> the door key.   forgot   lost   hid

8. It <u>started</u> on time.   played   showed   stopped

9. I have a <u>hard</u> bed.   big   soft   tiny

10. The movie is <u>short</u>.   long   funny   sad

11. I was <u>early</u> today.   home   lost   late

12. He drives too <u>fast</u>.   slow   hurry   far

Get the Picture

Look at each picture and sentence. One word in the sentence is wrong. Circle the wrong word. Then write the word that would make the sentence true.

 1. Pam is surprised because there is something in the box.

_____

- - - - - - - - - - -

nothing   everything

  2. The plane will leave at one o'clock.

_____

- - - - - - - - - - -

runway   arrive

 3. Tim doesn't know that there is a bee on the front of his shirt.

_____

- - - - - - - - - - -

sleeve   back

 4. When you set the table, place the fork on the right side of the plate.

_____

- - - - - - - - - - -

left   same

 5. Kim is sad because she found the missing bunny.

_____

- - - - - - - - - - -

tired   happy

 6. He stayed in bed because he was well.

_____

- - - - - - - - - - -

sick   young

Brainwork! The words *never* and *always* are opposites. Make a safety poster which has an "always" and a "never" rule.

FS-32031 Reading Activities

I Meant to Say

Whoops!

Each sentence below was meant to say the opposite. Circle the incorrect word in each sentence. Choose a word from the Word Box to replace it. Rewrite the sentence using the new word.

Word Box					
sad	after	hard	odd	apart	borrow

1. I chipped a tooth on the soft candy.

   _____

   -

2. Three and five are even numbers.

   _____

   -

3. My puzzle pieces fell together.

   _____

   -

4. June comes before May.

   _____

   -

5. I was happy when my friend moved.

   _____

   -

6. May I lend your eraser?

   _____

   -

Brainwork! Write each of these words and its opposite: first, began, mean, give, same, young, noise, and always.

Name _____   Skill: Synonyms/Antonyms

Directions: Use a word from the box to write a synonym
or antonym for each word.

tardy	sad	jolly	big	frown	lower	yellow
fat	thin	quiet	lift	close	loud	break
mend	far	grin	stop	early	small	start

1. (antonym) happy   _____

2. (synonym) fix   _____

3. (synonym) noisy   _____

4. (antonym) raise   _____

5. (synonym) near   _____

6. (antonym) smile   _____

7. (antonym) fat   _____

8. (synonym) large   _____

9. (antonym) late   _____

10. (synonym) begin   _____

Directions: Write the correct missing word on the line.

1. My _____ Ted is six.

2. I _____ a hot dog.

3. _____ lost my key.

4. Comb your _____ .

5. I hurt my _____ arm.

6. Pick a _____ .

7. I went last _____ .

8. I _____ a baby bird.

9. My dog eats _____ .

10. Let's _____ the boat.

sun	son
ate	eight
eye	I
hair	hare
right	write
flour	flower
night	knight
see	sea
meat	meet
sale	sail

FS-32031 Reading Activities

Name _____ Skill: Homonyms

Directions: Match the words that sound the same.
Write the number beside the word it matches.

1. right	2. bear	3. dear	4. eight
5. cent	6. sea	7. I	8. flour
9. pear	10. so	11. blew	12. ring

____ eye   ____ write   ____ sew   ____ pair

____ wring   ____ deer   ____ bare   ____ flower

____ blue   ____ see   ____ ate   ____ scent

Which One?

Look at each pair of words in the Word Box. Read the clues carefully to find which word belongs in the puzzle.

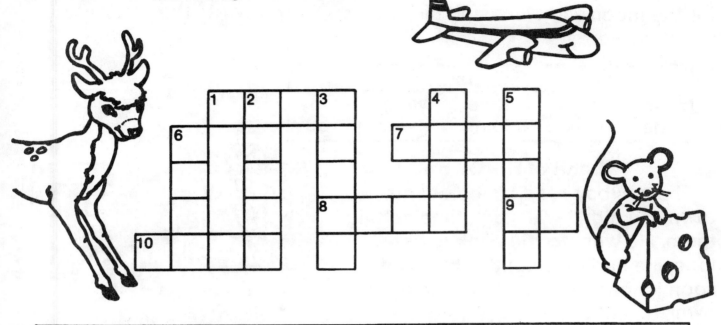

Word Box

| sale-sail | whole-hole | sent-cent | pair-pear | our-hour |
| dear-deer | plane-plain | no-know | write-right | ate-eight |

Across

1. an animal with antlers

7. to travel across water

8. 60 minutes of time

9. the opposite of yes

10. a penny

Down

2. the number before nine

3. the opposite of wrong

4. a set of two

5. a flying machine

6. an opening

Brainwork! Write a sentence to show the meaning of the unused word in each pair.

35   FS-32031 Reading Activities

The Right Words

Some words sound alike but have different spellings and meanings. Look at the pairs of words in the Word Box. Read the story below. Look for the incorrect words and circle them. Then rewrite the story using the right words.

Word Box				
road	waist	lone	weight	by
rode	waste	loan	wait	buy

Land of His Own

The cowboy road his horse into town. He didn't waist any time getting there. He went to the bank to get a lone. He had to weight awhile. But soon he had money to by land of his own!

Land of His Own

_____
- - - - - - - - - - - - - - - - - - -
_____
- - - - - - - - - - - - - - - - - - -
_____
- - - - - - - - - - - - - - - - - - -
_____
- - - - - - - - - - - - - - - - - - -
_____
- - - - - - - - - - - - - - - - - - -
_____
- - - - - - - - - - - - - - - - - - -
_____

Brainwork! Write a story using one word from each pair of words in the Word Box. Be sure to use the word with the right meaning.

Name _____

Write the letter that comes **before** the letter in the box. Put it **above** to find the answer to the riddle.

1. Which American president wore the largest hat?

u	i	f

p	o	f

x	j	u	i

u	i	f

m	b	s	h	f	t	u

i	f	b	e

2. Life is tough . . . but what can you always count on?

z	p	v	s

g	j	o	h	f	s	t

3. What animal can fly higher than a house?

b	m	m

p	g

u	i	f	n

—

i	p	v	t	f	t

d	b	o	u

g	m	z

4. What time is it when a clock strikes 13?

u	j	n	f

u	p

h	f	u

b

o	f	x

d	m	p	d	l

5. What is the oldest piece of furniture in the world?

u	i	f

n	v	m	u	j	q	m	j	d	b	u	j	p	o

u	b	c	m	f

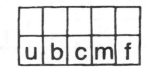

FS-32031 Reading Activities

Name _____

Write the letter that comes after the letter in the box. Put it below to find the answer to the riddle.

1. **What is the best way to keep goats from smelling?**

b	t	s		n	e	e		s	g	d	h	q		m	n	r	d	r

2. **What is the worst weather for rats and mice?**

v	g	d	m		h	s		q		h	m	r		b		s	r		m	c
									a						a				a	

c	n	f	r

3. **Why do monsters like to live in dark places?**

v	g	n		j	m	n	v	r		s	g		s	r		s	g	d
								?						a				

v		x		l	n	m	r	s	d	q	r		q	d
	a												a	

4. **What is gray?**

	l	d	k	s	d	c		o	d	m	f	t	h	m
a														

5. **What is red and round and goes putt putt?**

	m		n	t	s	a	n		q	c			o	o	k	d
a										a		a				

FS-32031 Reading Activities

RESIDENCE OF
V. SCARY MONSTER, ESQ.

Secret Alphabet Messages

Find the secret message.

Under each letter, write the letter that comes next in the alphabet.

Q	D	Z	C	H	M	F
		A				

O	T	Y	Y	K	D	R

Z	M	C
A		

F	Z	L	D	R
	A			

Z	Q	D
A		

E	T	M
			.

Under each letter, write the letter that comes before it in the alphabet.

X	I	J	D	I

E	P

Z	P	V

M	J	L	F

C	F	U	U	F	S
						___

S	F	B	E	J	O	H

P	S

N	B	U	I
				?

Brainwork! Create a different alphabet code. Write a short message and directions for decoding it. Give it to a friend to decode.

39

Name _____

Write the letter that comes **between** the letter above and below to find the answer to the riddle.

1. **Why did the giraffe stand on his head?**

s	n
u	p

s	q	h	o
u	s	j	q

b	t	q	h	n	t	r
d	v	s	j	p	v	t

a	h	q	c	r
c	j	s	e	t

2. **Why do elephants paint their toenails purple?**

r	n
t	p

s	g	d	x
u	i	f	z

b		m
	a	
d	b	o

g	h	c	d
i	j	e	f

h	m
j	o

f	q		o	d
		a		
h	s	b	q	f

u	h	m	d	r
w	j	o	f	t

3. **What is green and brown and crawls through the grass?**

a
b

f	h	q	k
h	j	s	m

r	b	n	t	s
t	d	p	v	u

v	g	n
x	i	p

c	q	n	o	o	d	c
e	s	p	q	q	f	e

g	d	q
i	f	s

b	n	n	j	h	d
d	p	p	l	j	f

4. **What has a brown jacket and goes 120 miles per hour?**

a
b

e	t	d	k
g	v	f	m

h	m	i	d	b	s	d	c
j	o	k	f	d	u	f	e

o	n	s		s	n
			a		
q	p	u	b	u	p

FS-32031 Reading Activities

Name _____

Put the words in ABC order on the _____. Start at the top with number 1.

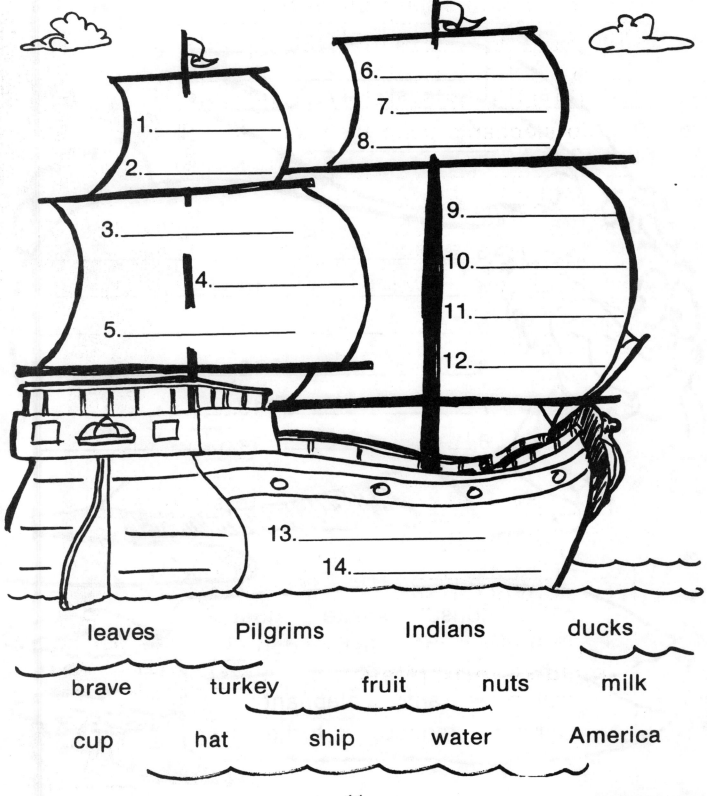

1. _____
2. _____
3. _____
4. _____
5. _____
6. _____
7. _____
8. _____
9. _____
10. _____
11. _____
12. _____
13. _____
14. _____

leaves   Pilgrims   Indians   ducks

brave   turkey   fruit   nuts   milk

cup   hat   ship   water   America

FS-32031 Reading Activities

Name _____

Put the words in ABC order on the _____ . Start at the top with number 1.

1. _____

2. _____

3. _____   9. _____

4. _____   10. _____

5. _____   11. _____

6. _____   12. _____

7. _____   13. _____

8. _____   14. _____

cat   mouse   snake   goat

hippo   rat   fish   dog

zebra   ant   elephant

bear   kangaroo   turtle

42

FS-32031 Reading Activities

Name _____

Choose the **word** that **completes** the ABC order of the sentence.

1. All baby spiders take _____ .

baths
vacations

2. A bear hibernates_____ .

days
months

3. Ducks swim _____ .

well
fast

4. A bee can_____ .

buzz
sting

5. Jane's monkey _____ .

jumps
plays

6. Big horses _____ .

canter
trot

I LOVE
TO SWIM!

7. Elephants have _____ .

feet
trunks

8. Lions run _____ .

wild
fast

9. All hippos _____ .

sleep
bite

10. Big dogs _____ .

bark
howl

11. Many otters play _____ .

ball
wildly

12. African giraffes like _____ .

trees
fruit

43

Name _____

Draw a line through the row in ABC order.
You may go ➡ ⬇ or ↘ .

bean	apple	you
zebra	bread	up
dog	cake	ant

desk	train	send
red	fish	are
good	cat	lion

see	take	red
flap	try	ask
Nan	bee	zoo

run	me	see
go	jump	push
find	down	look

two	some	violin
wild	very	corn
one	zebra	eat

sing	you	take
watch	yes	zing
box	toe	swing

44

FS-32031 Reading Activities

Name _____

Draw a line through the row in ABC order.
You may go ➡️⬇️ or ↘️.

cup	file	bed
run	desk	and
boy	arm	lamp

rose	back	key
name	quilt	very
price	born	run

Sue	card	we
red	two	wind
three	bee	can

floor	jump	elves
sun	hen	black
more	bear	Jack

stay	paper	she
no	rub	baby
up	win	the

page	rabbit	come
baby	rub	apple
trunk	money	veil

FS-32031 Reading Activities

Name _____

Find the word that is **out of order** in each numbered picture.
Write **that word** in the **same numbered** blank at the bottom to
find the mystery sentence.

1
we
down
every
he
lion

2
lose
men
picked
now
owl

3
umbrella
witch
youth
zoom
the

4
blue
orange
red
yellow
purple

5
cross
garden
hippo
flowers
line

1 _____ 2 _____ 3 _____ 4 _____ 5 _____

46

Name _____

Find the word that is **out of order** in each numbered picture. Write **that word** in the **same numbered** blank at the bottom to find the mystery sentence.

1. apple
   dogs
   fire
   gold
   cats

2. take
   violet
   word
   yellow
   have

3. angry
   down
   very
   elephant
   four

4. bear
   candy
   soft
   help
   ice

5. paper
   quiz
   rat
   two
   fur

1 _____ 2 _____ 3 _____ 4 _____ 5 _____ .

47

Name _____

Find the word that is **out of order** in each numbered picture. Write **that word** in the **same numbered** blank at the top to find the mystery sentence.

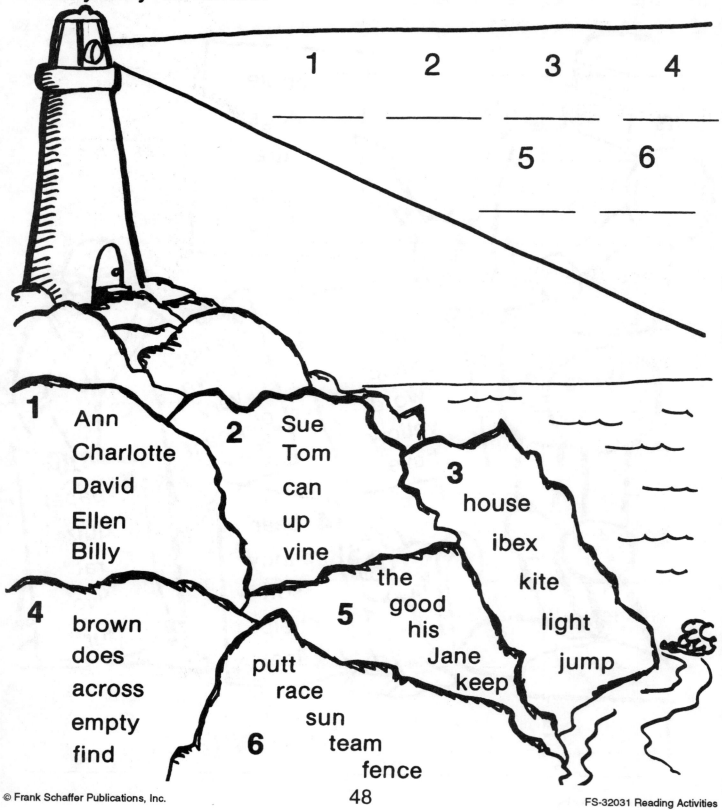

1 ____ 2 ____ 3 ____ 4 ____

5 ____ 6 ____

1
Ann
Charlotte
David
Ellen
Billy

2
Sue
Tom
can
up
vine

3
house
ibex
kite
light
jump

4
brown
does
across
empty
find

5
the
good
his
Jane
keep

6
putt
race
sun
team
fence

FS-32031 Reading Activities

Name _____

Put the words in ABC order to make a sentence.

1. steel makes blast furnace A

   _____ .

2. white dog Amy's is

   _____ .

3. tails long Cats have

   _____ .

4. sizes Bears in come many

   _____ .

5. seeds eat Chickens gray

   _____ .

6. regularly peanuts eats Bob

   _____ .

7. word notice Frank might one

   _____ .

8. wilt leaves may Green

   _____ .

9. picture draws Chris every

   _____ .

SIZE **AA** BEAR

SIZE **A** BEAR

BARELY **A** BEAR

Name _____

Put the words in ABC order to make a sentence.

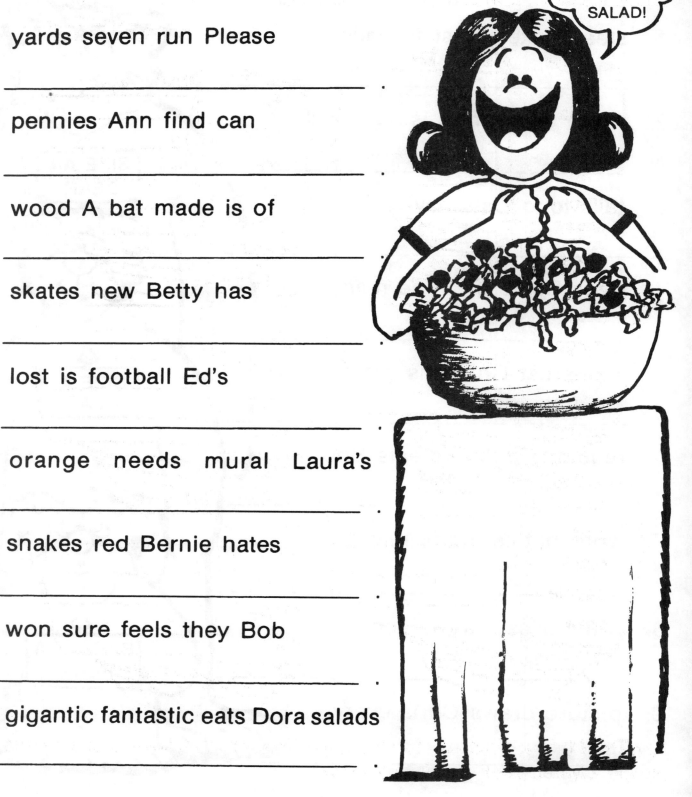

1. yards seven run Please

    _____ .

2. pennies Ann find can

    _____ .

3. wood A bat made is of

    _____ .

4. skates new Betty has

    _____ .

5. lost is football Ed's

    _____ .

6. orange   needs   mural   Laura's

    _____ .

7. snakes red Bernie hates

    _____ .

8. won sure feels they Bob

    _____ .

9. gigantic fantastic eats Dora salads

    _____ .

50   FS-32031 Reading Activities

Name _____

Write each group of words in alphabetical order.
Look at the second letter of each word to help you.

day
deck
dock

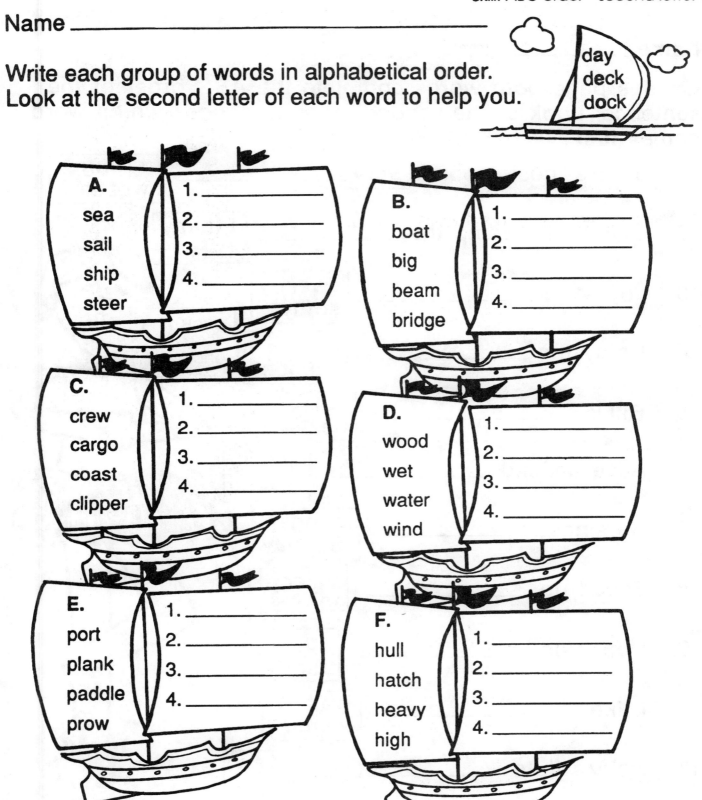

A.
sea
sail
ship
steer

1. _____
2. _____
3. _____
4. _____

B.
boat
big
beam
bridge

1. _____
2. _____
3. _____
4. _____

C.
crew
cargo
coast
clipper

1. _____
2. _____
3. _____
4. _____

D.
wood
wet
water
wind

1. _____
2. _____
3. _____
4. _____

E.
port
plank
paddle
prow

1. _____
2. _____
3. _____
4. _____

F.
hull
hatch
heavy
high

1. _____
2. _____
3. _____
4. _____

Try This! Use a dictionary to write definitions for the following ship words:
bridge, clipper, deck, hatch, hull, prow.

51

Name _____

On this page both words complete the ABC order of the sentence. Look at the second letter to choose which word comes **first**.

1. John's music sounds very _____ .
   wrong
   western

2. Ballet can cramp the _____ .
   tummy
   toes

3. Joy sang _____ .
   sweetly
   softly

4. I play the _____ .
   tuba
   trumpet

5. Bill is _____ .
   noisy
   neat

6. Alice danced _____ .
   slowly
   swiftly

7. He sings _____ .
   songs
   Sunday

8. Speed up _____ !
   Valerie
   Virginia

9. Hop, skip, _____ .
   trip
   tumble

10. I like to _____ .
    waltz
    wiggle

11. Betty's flute is _____ .
    new
    nice

12. Al's band makes _____ .
    music
    money

OOCH OUCH EECH ORCH!

Name _____

Put the words in ABC order to make a sentence. Look at the second letter if two words start the same.

1. silver I skies see

   _____ .

2. caught Bob crawfish Louisiana in

   _____ .

3. monsters How many watches own?

   _____ ?

4. washing is windows Ira

   _____ .

5. roses red My terrific smell

   _____ .

6. sleepy A snail wakes sometimes

   _____ .

7. ten Joe tapped turtles tiny

   _____ .

8. Lucy mellow Lazy music makes

   _____

IT'S TIME TO SCARE PEOPLE

Name _____

Draw a line through the row in ABC order.
You may go ➡ ⬇ or ↘ .

sad	step	speech
so	set	sip
sit	sun	soap

be	buy	bow
big	bag	best
bug	bring	but

help	hide	hug
hurt	hat	horse
hinge	hard	him

mine	my	mud
mush	mail	milk
me	mitt	mug

rub	rush	risk
rat	red	rule
rung	rag	read

lap	look	leaf
limp	love	lab
let	lag	lump

Name _____

Put the words in ABC order on the _____. Look at the second and third letters if the words start the same. Start with number 1.

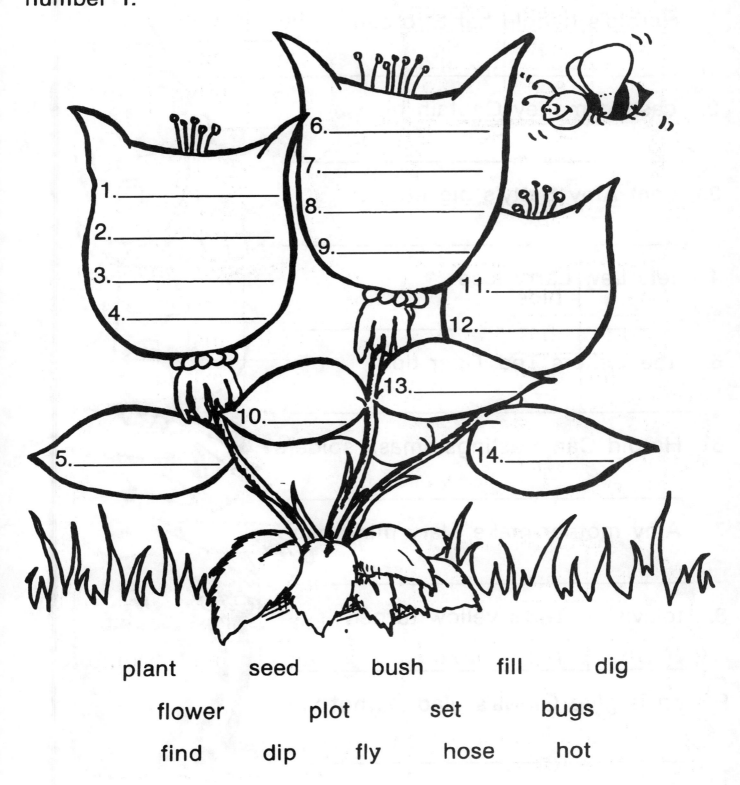

1. _____

2. _____

3. _____

4. _____

5. _____

6. _____

7. _____

8. _____

9. _____

10. _____

11. _____

12. _____

13. _____

14. _____

plant	seed	bush	fill	dig
flower	plot	set	bugs	
find	dip	fly	hose	hot

FS-32031 Reading Activities

Name _____

Put the words in ABC order to make a sentence. Look at the second and third letters if two words start the same.

1. Harold's handle hat Bob can

   _____ .

2. cashed money Captain his Carl

   _____ .

3. bent Amy Betty's big buckle

   _____ .

4. lets Lew Larry lose

   _____ .

5. the waiters Ted Tiger tips

   _____ .

6. Harold Can Hastings smash spiders?

   _____ ?

7. Amy mother make Mary mind can

   _____ .

8. television Ted's yellow turned

   _____ .

9. on is glue Gloria's glad Be not you

   _____ .

Go-Togethers

Look at each group of words below. First cross out the word that does not belong. Then add a word from the Word Box that does belong.

Word Box

refrigerator   sweater   fountain   towel   scissors   shovel

1.

paper	pencil
eraser	stapler
penguin	glue

_____

2.

toothbrush	sausage
mirror	sink
soap	washcloth

_____

3.

pans	stove
dishes	cupboard
globe	toaster

_____

4.

shirts	soil
skirts	shoes
pants	socks

_____

5.

chocolate	hose
lawnmower	tools
paint	clippers

_____

6.

swings	benches
pond	flowers
grass	pound

_____

Brainwork! For each list above complete this title: "Things You'd Find In..."

Whirl-a-Word Puzzles

The puzzles below contain the names of four instruments used for seeing. Follow the directions to discover the name of each instrument.

Begin at the ★. Count every two letters and circle the letter. Then write the circled letters in the correct order on the blanks below the puzzle.

1.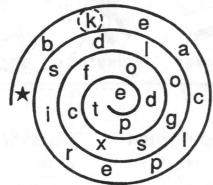

_____ _____

2.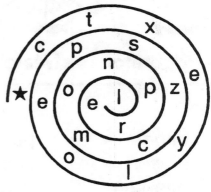

_____ _____

3.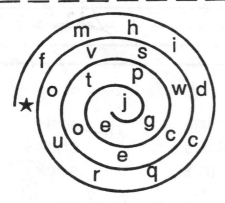

_____ _____

4.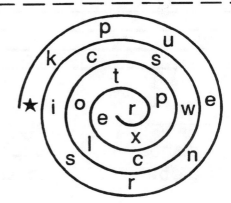

_____ _____

Write the correct word from above in each sentence.

A. The scientist looked through the _____ at the strands of hair.

B. The astronomer looked through the _____ to see the planet in the night sky.

C. The children squealed with delight as the patterns

changed in the _____ .

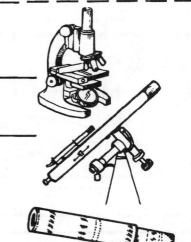

Brainwork! Create a whirl-a-word puzzle using a word 10 to 12 letters long.

Kaleidoscope Fun

Rearrange the letters in each circle to make two or three words.
Write the letters in the boxes below the circle.

Brainwork! Some words are spelled the same forward and backward like the word *mom*. Think of three more words like this. Write them.

   FS-32031 Reading Activities

Kaleidoscope Game

Rearrange the letters in each circle to make two or three words.
Write the letters in the boxes below the circle.

Brainwork! Draw a circle. Write in the letters *t, s, e, a, k*. Make two words with those letters.

Name Puzzle

Write your **first** name in the boxes below. Write one
letter to a box. If there's room, write your **middle** name.
Then make as many words from these letters as you can.

☐ ☐ ☐ ☐ ☐ ☐ ☐ ☐ ☐ ☐ ☐ ☐ ☐

_____ _____ _____ _____

_____ _____ _____ _____

_____ _____ _____ _____

_____ _____ _____ _____

Write your **last** name in the boxes below. Write one letter to a box. If
there's room, write your **middle** name. Then make as many words from
these letters as you can.

☐ ☐ ☐ ☐ ☐ ☐ ☐ ☐ ☐ ☐ ☐ ☐ ☐

_____ _____ _____ _____

_____ _____ _____ _____

_____ _____ _____ _____

_____ _____ _____ _____

Write three sentences using at least four of the words you made above.

_____

_____

_____

_____

Brainwork! Make another name puzzle like the one above. Use the name
of someone in your school.

Puzzles in a Pocket

1. Write the names of the pictures in the boxes.
   Use one box for each letter.
2. Write each circled letter in one of the circles below.
3. Unscramble the letters to form a new word and write it on the line.
   Use the picture clues below to help you.

A.

Chick

chalk

chain

cihan

china

B.

C.

D.

Brainwork! Write the names of three things that will fit in a pocket. Use words that begin with *pl, bl, ch,* or *sh*.

 FS-32031 Reading Activities

Pocket Puzzles

1. Write the names of the pictures in the boxes.
   Use one box for each letter.
2. Write each circled letter in one of the circles below.
3. Unscramble the letters to form a new word and write it on the line.
   Use the picture clues below to help you.

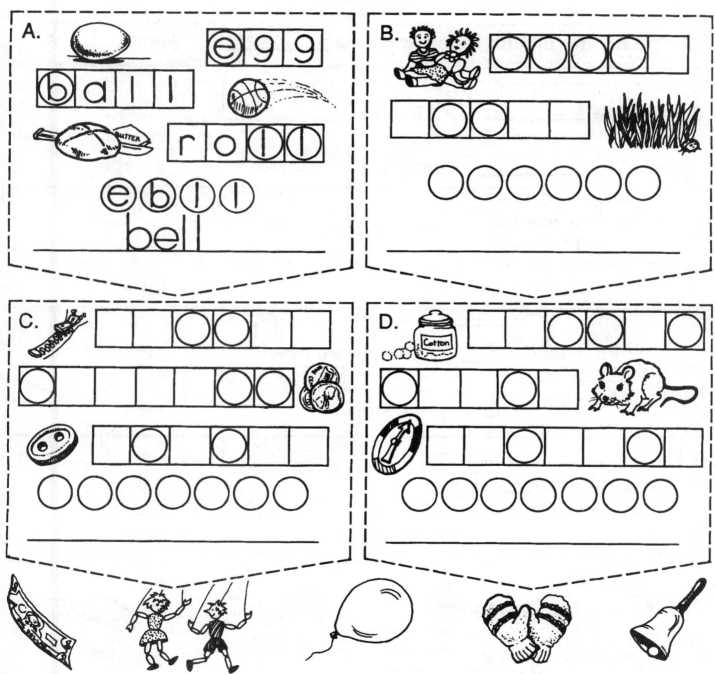

Brainwork! Write the names of three things too large to fit in a pocket.
Use words that have double letters in them.

Name_____

Pattern Pairs

Write the correct word from each pair to complete each sentence.

1. There is a _____ tree in the yard.   pin

2. You can hold cloth together with a _____ .   pine

3. I need a _____ of cloth.   scrap

4. I got a _____ when I fell.   scrape

5. The _____ puppy wanted to play.   cut

6. I _____ the paper in half.   cute

7. The bird likes to _____ on the window.   tap

8. Use _____ to hold up the sign.   tape

9. The apple was _____ .   rip

10. I got a _____ in my new jacket.   ripe

11. We _____ to take a trip there.   plan

12. Grandpa came on a _____ .   plane

Brainwork! Choose a pair of sentences above to copy and illustrate.

64   FS-32031 Reading Activities

Word Detective

Be a word detective. Use the clues in the Clue Box to help you decode the boldfaced words and answer the questions.

Clue Box	
uni- one	**tri-** three
bi- two	**dec-** ten
cent- one hundred	

1. How many years in a **century**?

2. How many wheels on a **bicycle**?

3. How many angles in a **triangle**?

4. How many years in a **decade**?

5. How many legs on a **centipede**?

6. How many horns on a **unicorn**?

7. How many years in a **centennial**?

8. How many wheels on a **unicycle**?

9. How many legs on a **decapod**?

10. How many horns on a **triceratops**?

Brainwork! Draw and label a unicycle, a bicycle, a tricycle. Write which you think would be the hardest to ride and why.

Name_____

Coded Tongue Twisters

Samuel Morse invented the telegraph and the Morse Code. Morse Code is a series of dots and dashes used to send messages on the telegraph.

Use the Code Box to decode the tongue twisters below.

Morse Code Box	
A	•—
B	—•••
C	—•—•
D	—••
E	•
F	••—•
G	——•
H	••••
I	••
J	•———
K	—•—
L	•—••
M	——
N	—•
O	———
P	•——•
Q	——•—
R	•—•
S	•••
T	—
U	••—
V	•••—
W	•——
X	—••—
Y	—•——
Z	——••

1. •— —•/•—••/•/•—/•••/• •— —•/••/—•—•/—•—

   _____   _____

•— •— —•/••/•/—•—•/• ———/••—•

___ _____   _____

•— —•/••/——•/——•/•— •—/—•/——•

_____   _____

•— —•/•—/•••/••• ••/— ———/—•

_____   _____   _____

2. •••/••—/•••/•—/—•

   _____

•••/—•/•—/—•—•/—•—/••• ———/—•

_____   _____

•••/•—/—•/•—•/——/••/—•/•••/•/•••

_____

———/••• •••/•—/•—•—••/—/—•——

_____   _____

•••/•—/•—•/—••/••/—•/•/•••

_____

Brainwork! Choose a letter and use it to write a tongue twister. Write your tongue twister in Morse Code.

FS-32031 Reading Activities

Alphabet Code Puzzle

Make a code wheel by cutting out the two wheels and fastening them with a brad. Then turn the wheels so the **A** on the outside wheel is in line with **z** on the inside wheel.

A becomes **z**, **B** becomes **y**.

Next, complete the Reverse Code Box.

Finally, decode these names of family members.

1. nlgsvi _____

2. uzgsvi _____

3. yilgsvi _____

4. hrhgvi _____

5. kvg _____

6. tizmwnlgsvi _____

7. tizmwuzgsvi _____

Reverse Code Box	
A	z
B	
C	
D	
E	
F	
G	
H	
I	
J	
K	
L	
M	
N	
O	
P	
Q	
R	
S	
T	
U	
V	
W	
X	
Y	
Z	

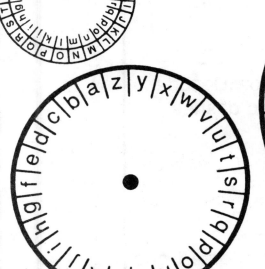

sample

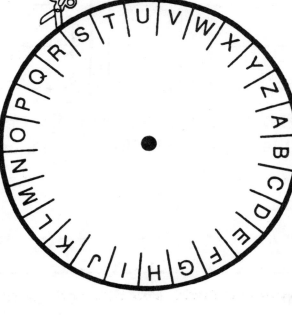

Bag the Categories

Look carefully at the symbols used for Morse Code
in the Code Box.

Fill the shopping bags with the correct letters.

Example:

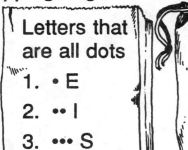

Letters that
are all dots

1. • E

2. •• I

3. ••• S

4. •••• H

Letters that
are all dashes

1. _____

2. _____

3. _____

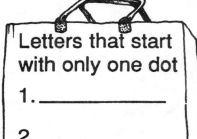

Letters that start
with only one dot

1._____

2._____

3._____

4._____

5._____

6._____

Letters that start
with only one dash

1._____

2._____

3._____

4._____

5._____

6._____

7._____

Morse Code Box
A • –
B – • • •
C – • – •
D – • •
E •
F • • – •
G – – •
H • • • •
I • •
J • – – –
K – • –
L • – • •
M – –
N – •
O – – –
P • – – •
Q – – • –
R • – •
S • • •
T –
U • • –
V • • • –
W • – –
X – • • –
Y – • – –
Z – – • •

Use the Code Box to decode the message below. Decode
by substituting the correct letter for the dots and dashes.

– / •••• / •• / •••   •• / •••

_____ _____

– – / – – – / • – • / ••• / •   – • – • / – – – / – •• / •

_____ _____

Brainwork! List five of your favorite pets using Morse Code.
Trade lists with a friend and decode each other's list.

FS-32031 Reading Activities

Riddles and Codes

Use the code to write the correct letter below each symbol.
You will discover the answers to some riddles.

Code Box

Example: What goes up to the door but never goes in?

T H E   S T E P S

1. What side of your house is the best side for planting a tree?

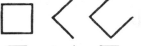

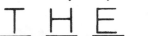

2. What holds water yet is full of holes?

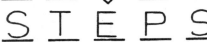

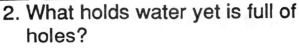

3. What goes up when the rain comes down?

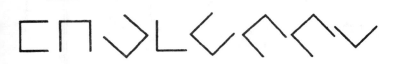

4. What grows in winter and dies in summer and has its roots upwards?

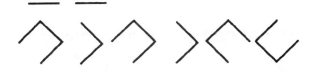

Brainwork! Use the code above to write your favorite riddle. Give it to a friend to decode and answer.

Codes and Riddles

Use the code to write the correct letter below each symbol.
You will discover the answers to some riddles.

Code Box

 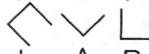

Example: What gets lost every time you stand up?

<u>Y</u> <u>O</u> <u>U</u> <u>R</u>   <u>L</u> <u>A</u> <u>P</u>

1. What is the first thing you put in a garden?

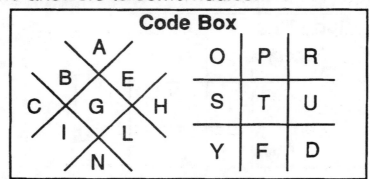

___ ___ ___ ___   ___ ___ ___ ___

2. What always goes to bed with its shoes on?

___ ___ ___ ___ ___

3. What kind of pine has the sharpest needles?

___ ___ ___ ___ ___ ___ ___ ___

4. What can you make that you can't use?

___ ___ ___ ___ ___

Brainwork! Use the code above to write five names.

70   FS-32031 Reading Activities

Quick Change Ladders

Can you change **one** letter in each word to make a new word?
Complete each step on the ladder. Use the words in the Word Box.

Word Box

bay	map	tan	dot	hog
cap	ten	ban	pat	hug	cot

Example:

pet
pat
sat

1. boy

   man

2. cat

   mop

3. tin

   man

4. dog

   cat

5. hop

   jug

Brainwork! Look up the word *cot* in the dictionary. Write its definition and use it in a sentence.

Quick Ladder Climb

Can you change one letter in each word to make a new word?
Complete each step on the ladder. Use the words in the Word Box.

Word Box

tell	halt	pest	poke
lean	pike	past	half
mean	tall	walk	wall

Example:

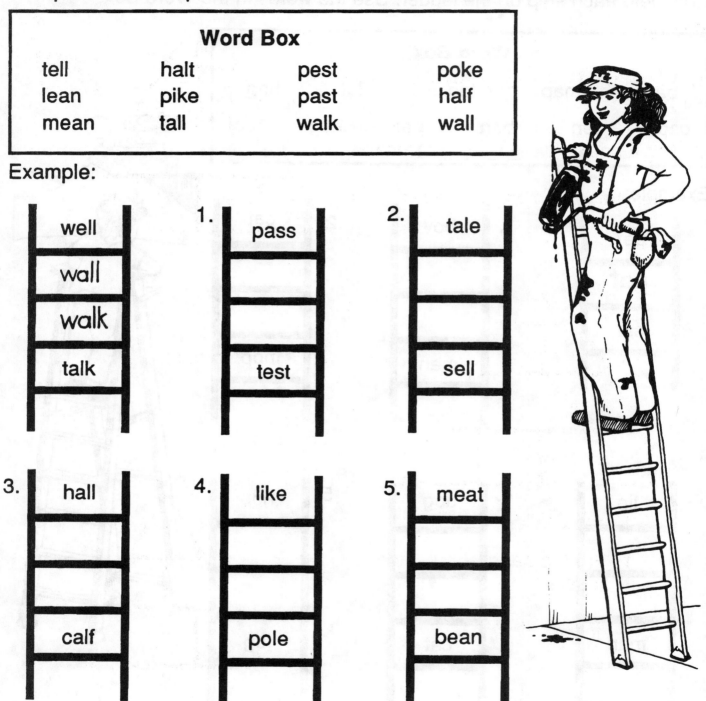

well
wall
walk
talk

1.
pass

test

2.
tale

sell

3.
hall

calf

4.
like

pole

5.
meat

bean

Brainwork! Choose one of the completed word ladders above and write a sentence using all the words on the ladder.

FS-32031 Reading Activities

Word Triangles

Complete the word triangles by adding one letter in each row to form a new word. Use the sentence clues to help you.

Example: **A** Triangle

1. We played _____ my friend's house.

2. For a snack, we _____ a fruit roll.

3. I watched the clock so I wouldn't be

   _____ .

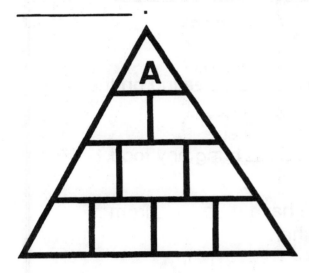

I Triangle

1. Put the sand _____ the bucket.

2. Is your bucket plastic or

   _____ ?

3. That bucket has a _____ of green.

A Triangle

1. Will you give me _____ apple?

2. Mitza _____ John will eat apples.

3. Let's build a _____ castle.

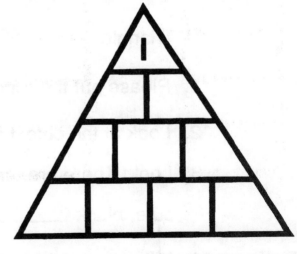

Brainwork! List ten words that use only the letters of the first half of the alphabet—**A** through **M**. Use your words in sentences.

73 FS-32031 Reading Activities

Word Triangles

Complete the word triangles by adding one letter in each row to form a new word. Use the clues to help you.

Example: O Triangle

1. Hop _____ the bus.

2. You are the _____.

3. Did you hear that _____?

O Triangle with letters:
O / O N / O N E / T O N E

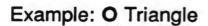

O Triangle

1. There is _____ eating on the bus.

2. I will _____ bring any food.

3. Today I have a _____ from my father.

U Triangle

1. Please put the window _____ .

2. Look at the cute, black _____ .

3. Look! There are three more

cut, black _____ .

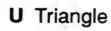

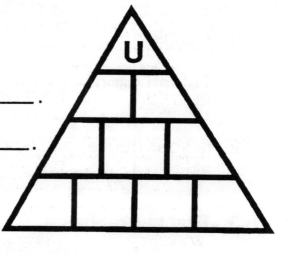

Brainwork! Write ten words that use only the letters of the second half of the alphabet—**N** through **Z**. Use your words in sentences.

Good Sports

Bill and Sara are brother and sister. They are on the same soccer team. Sara is an excellent kicker. **She**₁ scores many goals. Bill is a terrific goalie. Many times **he**₂ keeps the other team from scoring. Bill and Sara often hear their parents cheering **them**₃ on. They say **it**₄ helps them play their best. They don't always win the game, but **both**₅ always enjoy **it.**₆

Each numbered word in the story stands for the name of someone or something in the story. Decide what each word replaces. Write your answers on the lines below.

1. She— _____
   Bill   Sara

2. He— _____
   Bill   Sara

3. them— _____
   Bill and Sara   Bill and Sara's parents

4. it— _____
   scoring   cheering

5. both— _____
   Bill and Sara   Bill and Sara's parents

6. it— _____
   winning   the game

Brainwork! What sport do you enjoy playing or watching? Write about it.

What Does It Mean?

Choose a word from the Word Box to replace the boldfaced word in each sentence. Write it on the line. A dictionary can help you.

Word Box

shake brave smell copy little
strong tease choose disappear

1. The mouse felt **puny** standing next to the elephant.

2. Sour milk can have a bad **odor.**

3. I get mad when big kids **taunt** my sister.

4. The people will **elect** a new president.

5. It was so cold I began to **quiver.**

6. These trees look **sturdy** enough to climb.

7. I saw the light in the distance **vanish.**

8. My brother can **imitate** the sound of a bird.

9. The **courageous** knight fought the mean dragon.

Brainwork! Choose two of the sentences above to illustrate.

In Other Words

Choose a word from the Word Box to replace the boldfaced word in each sentence.

Let's exchange places.

Yes, let's Trade places.

Word Box

trade	smile	hit	shine	path
spin	move	burn	extra	dressed

1. She can really **whack** the ball. _____

2. The dancer began to **twirl.** _____

3. I couldn't **budge** the heavy box. _____

4. The teacher said to **exchange** papers. _____

5. The silly joke made him **grin.** _____

6. A hot iron can **scorch** clothes. _____

7. The **spare** tire is in the trunk. _____

8. We followed the **trail** back to camp. _____

9. Waxing the car made it **gleam.** _____

10. The king was **clad** in royal robes. _____

Brainwork! Write three sentences that might make a friend grin. Exchange papers and find out if they do!

Learning to Skate

Read this story about learning to skate. Then answer the questions.

Many times I had **longed** to be able to ice skate. Finally my big sister agreed to teach me.

I was filled with **glee** as I laced up my skates for the first time. I thought I would be **gliding** over the ice in minutes. Was I surprised when I stood up and fell right on the ice. It sure was **chilly**!

My sister helped me up and said, "Don't **fret**. After a few more **tumbles** you'll be skating like a star!"

1. Which boldfaced word in the story means:

a. cold? _____ d. worry? _____

b. wished? _____ e. moving? _____

c. joy? _____ f. falls? _____

2. Circle the best answer.

a. The word **chilly** has to do with

    food   temperature   skates

b. Which would most likely fill you with **glee**?

    being sick   a surprise party

c. Which would you most likely **long** for?

    a missing toy   a broken pencil

d. When would you be most likely to **fret**?

    if you missed the school bus   if you got a good grade

Brainwork! Draw and label five things that can glide through the air or on the water.

Which Is It?

Look at each pair of words below. They look almost the same but they have different meanings. Choose the correct word for each sentence. Fill in the ◯ above the word.

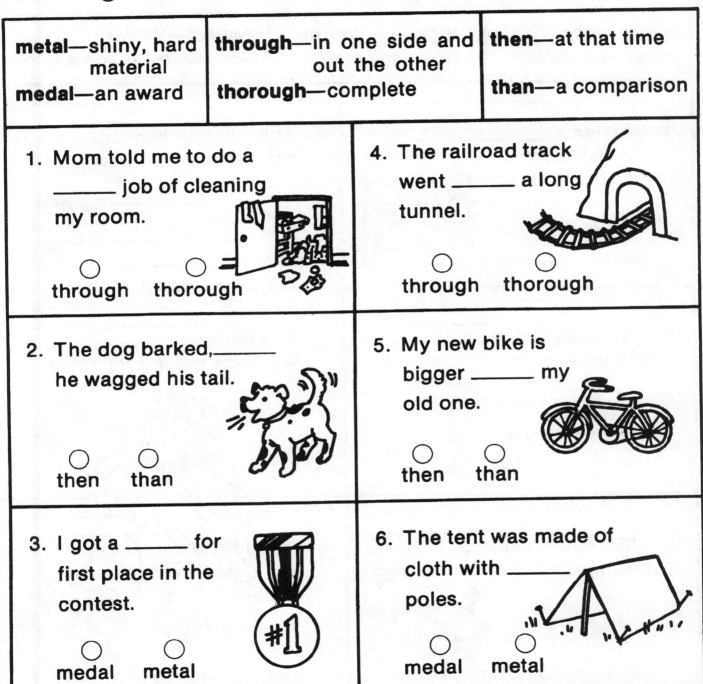

| **metal**—shiny, hard material | **through**—in one side and out the other | **then**—at that time |
| **medal**—an award | **thorough**—complete | **than**—a comparison |

1. Mom told me to do a _____ job of cleaning my room.

   ◯ through   ◯ thorough

4. The railroad track went _____ a long tunnel.

   ◯ through   ◯ thorough

2. The dog barked,_____ he wagged his tail.

   ◯ then   ◯ than

5. My new bike is bigger _____ my old one.

   ◯ then   ◯ than

3. I got a _____ for first place in the contest.

   ◯ medal   ◯ metal

6. The tent was made of cloth with _____ poles.

   ◯ medal   ◯ metal

Brainwork! Use each pair of words in a sentence. Example: I used to be shorter **than** my sister, but **then** I grew!

79   FS-32031 Reading Activities

Not Quite

Some words look very much alike but have different meanings. Look at the words and their meanings below. Then choose the correct word for each sentence. Fill in the ○ above the word and write it on the line.

| quite—very | loose—not tight | guest—visitor |
| quiet—not noisy | lose—misplace | guessed—made a guess |

1. We had a _____ for dinner.
   ○ guest   ○ guessed

2. I promise not to _____ the note.
   ○ loose   ○ lose

3. The children kept _____ during the fire drill.
   ○ quite   ○ quiet

4. The weather was _____ hot yesterday.
   ○ quite   ○ quiet

5. The children _____ who was behind the mask.
   ○ guest   ○ guessed

6. My tooth was _____ so I didn't want to eat an apple.
   ○ lose   ○ loose

Brainwork! "I **guessed** we were having a **guest**." Write sentences using the other two pairs of words from the Word Box.

A Close Call

Look at the words and meanings below. Choose the correct word to complete each sentence. Then write the meaning of the word you chose on the line below the sentence.

 **desert**—very dry land

dessert—after-meal treat

1. Dad made us pudding for a _____

   special _____ .

   _____

2. We drove across miles of _____

   sandy _____ .

   _____

 **lose**—misplace

loose—not tight

3. My brother's sweater was

   too _____ .

   _____

4. The money is in my pocket so I

   won't _____ it.

   _____

 **single**—only, one

signal—warning sign

5. The _____ letter
   in the mailbox was for me.

   _____

6. The red light was a _____
   to stop.

   _____

Brainwork! What can't you do with a door? Clothes it! Write two riddles like this using the words **picture** and **pitcher**.

Different Meanings

Look at the list below. Two different meanings are given for each word.

sign	1) a symbol	2) to write your name
dash	1) a small amount	2) to run quickly
chief	1) leader	2) first or main
trip	1) journey	2) to stumble
quarter	1) one-fourth	2) 25¢ coin
company	1) visitor or guests	2) business

Decide which meaning the boldfaced word has in each sentence below. Fill in ① or ②. Then write the meaning on the line.

① ② A. Be careful not to **trip** over the rock!

_____
_ _
_____

① ② B. We are having **company** tonight.

_____
_ _
_____

① ② C. When it started to rain we made a **dash** for the house.

_____
_ _
_____

① ② D. They turned left at the stop **sign.**

_____
_ _
_____

① ② E. Mom gave me a **quarter** for my piggy bank.

_____
_ _
_____

① ② F. The **chief** of police spoke to us about safety.

_____
_ _
_____

Brainwork! Write a new sentence for every boldfaced word. Have each sentence show the word's other meaning.

FS-32031 Reading Activities

Which Scale?

Read these different meanings for the word **scale**.

1) thin plates on reptiles or fish.
2) an object used to measure weight
3) to climb up the side
4) a map marking for distance
5) a group of musical notes

1. Which meaning of **scale** (1, 2, 3, 4, or 5) does each picture show?

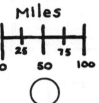

○   ○   ○   ○   ○

2. Choose the correct meaning of **scale** in each sentence. Write the meaning on the line below the sentence.

A. The **scale** shows that the town is 15 miles away.

_____

B. Many dinosaurs had **scales**.

_____

C. I can play **scales** on the piano.

_____

D. She put the meat on a **scale**.

_____

E. He **scaled** the high mountain.

_____

Brainwork! Look up the word **mark** in a dictionary. Write five of its meanings.

Word Puzzler

Read the words in the Word Box.

1.

2.

3.

4.

5.

6.

7.

8.

Word Box

Three
one
Four
eight
two
Seven
six
five

Find the correct word from the Word Box for each sentence. Write the word in the boxes above. The correct word has the same number of letters as there are boxes.

1. Do you know the story of The ____ Little Pigs?

2. ____ and four are eight.

3. Which one of the ____ puzzles do you want—the large one or the small one?

4. Three and three are ____.

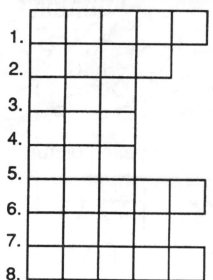

5. Today is the baby's first birthday; she is ____ year old.

6. Do you like to play ____ Up?

7. Mom says to be home for dinner by ____ o'clock.

8. I go to bed at ____ o'clock.

Brainwork! On the back of this paper, write the number words in order from *one* to *ten*.

FS-32031 Reading Activities

Word Puzzler

Read the words in the Word Box.

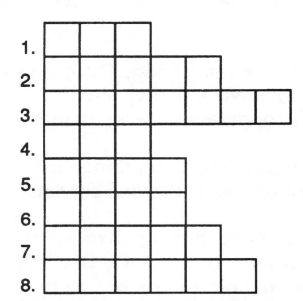

Word Box

count
add
numbers
plus
minus
equals
even
odd

Find the correct word from the Word Box for each sentence. Write the word in the boxes above. The correct word has the same number of letters as there are boxes.

1. Begin at one and count to nineteen using ____ numbers.

2. If you begin at one, how high can you ____ ?

3. Fill in the chart with the ____ from 1 to 1000.

4. If you ____ six and two, you will have eight.

5. Two ____ six equals eight .

6. Begin at two and count to twenty using ____ numbers.

7. Three ____ one equals two.

8. Three minus one ____ two .

Brainwork! Write one problem using some of the words in the Word Box.

Needs and Wants

Read this story about working together. The boldfaced words may be new to you. Their meanings are given below the story. Write the word that matches each meaning.

People everywhere have the same needs. They all need food, clothing, and shelter to **survive**, or stay alive.

In a community people **cooperate**, or work together, to get the things they need.

Some people provide **goods**, which are things made or grown for people to use. Other people provide **services**, or jobs that help others.

Besides needs, there are many things people want to make their lives more comfortable or fun. They buy many goods and services to enjoy in their **leisure**, or free time.

1. _____ work together

2. _____ free time

3. _____ stay alive

4. _____ things made or grown for people to use

5. _____ jobs people do for each other

The pictures show jobs people do. Label them **goods** or **services**.

A. _____

B. _____

Brainwork! Draw and label ten pictures of goods and services you use.

Looking for Energy

Read this story about energy. The boldfaced words may be new to you. Their meanings are given below the story. Write the word that matches each meaning.

Scientists are looking for new **sources**, or places, to get energy. They are finding new ways to make, or **produce**, the power we will need in the future.

One kind of energy is **geothermal**. "Geo" means "earth" and "thermal" means "heat." Geothermal energy comes from heat that is already stored inside the earth.

Another kind of energy is **solar**. "Sol" means "sun." The sunlight is changed into energy we can use.

1. _____ heat from the earth

2. _____ from the sun

3. _____ to make

4. _____ places to get something

These pictures show kinds of energy. Label them **geothermal** or **solar**.

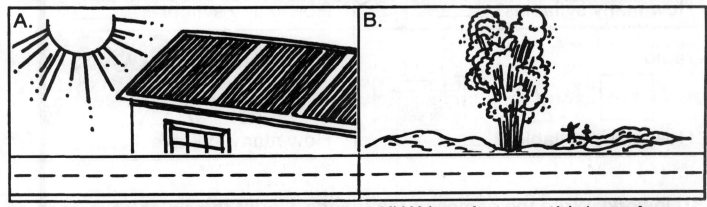

Brainwork! "-ology" means "the study of." Write what you think **geology** means. Then write the dictionary definition.

Count Down

You can **see** ☐3☐ vowels in the word **pancake**.

You can **hear** only △2△ vowel sounds in the word **pancake**.

The number of syllables in a word is the same as the number of vowels you hear in the word.

Remember! Every syllable has a vowel sound.

☐ = vowels I see   △ = vowels I hear

playground	magic
☐3☐ △2△	☐ △
How many syllables? __2__	How many syllables? ____

dinosaur	peanut
☐ △	☐ △
How many syllables? ____	How many syllables? ____

locomotive	unlock
☐ △	☐ △
How many syllables? ____	How many syllables? ____

radio	children
☐ △	☐ △
How many syllables? ____	How many syllables? ____

Brainwork! Write the names of ten friends. Count the syllables in each name and write the number.

FS-32031 Reading Activities

A Single Syllable

Remember! A word with one syllable is never divided. A word with one syllable may have one or more vowels.
Write the one-syllable word that completes the riddle.

1. What kind of fish can you find in a bird cage?

    parrot   perch   tuna

    _____

2. What has hands but no fingers?

    kitten   clock   boat

    _____

3. What has teeth but never eats?

    tiger   rug   comb

    _____

4. What bird is a letter of the alphabet?

    robin   jay   bee

    _____

5. What goes through glass without breaking it?

    light   baseball   egg

    _____

6. What falls all the time but never gets hurt?

    girl   toothbrush   snow

    _____

7. What is full of holes and still holds water?

    sponge   bucket   peach

    _____

8. What smells the best in a bakery?

    pan   popcorn   nose

    _____

Brainwork! Write a list of one-syllable words that you can make from the letters in the word **friendship**. List more than ten.

FS-32031 Reading Activities

Prefixes Are Syllables

Remember! When a word has a prefix,
the word is divided between the
prefix and the base word.
Example: re-turn

Circle the word that has a prefix. Write the word, using a hyphen to
divide it into syllables.

1. My little sister is in preschool. _____

2. Mom unlocked the garage door. _____

3. Grandpa watched the replay. _____

4. Aunt Susan will unwrap the box. _____

5. My brother reset the clock. _____

6. Dad drinks nonfat milk. _____

7. The twins look alike. _____

8. I like to ride the subway. _____

9. Uncle Joe can explain this math. _____

10. Grandma will repaint my bike. _____

11. My cousin went indoors. _____

12. Theresa likes to explore. _____

Brainwork! List at least six words that have the prefix **un.**

A Suffix Is a Syllable

Remember! When a word has a suffix, the word is divided between the base word and the suffix.

Example: clear-ly

Write the word that makes sense in the sentence, dividing it into syllables. Use a hyphen.

rested	making	farmer	lumpy	sweeten
seedless	healthful	peaches	spoonful	boxes

1. Alice picked some ripe _____ for Grandmother.

2. That _____ grows strawberries, too.

3. These berries will _____ my cereal.

4. Dad is _____ a tasty banana bread.

5. Tracy likes _____ grapes the best.

6. An orange is a _____ dessert.

7. Put a _____ of blueberries in the batter.

8. Bill likes raisins; they make his oatmeal _____ .

9. I can help you put the apples in _____ .

10. After picking cherries, we _____ .

Brainwork! Describe yourself using four words that have suffixes.

Word Bank

Write each word in the correct part of the piggy bank, dividing it into syllables. Use a hyphen.

windy	floating	subway	rewrite
fearless	unclear	hilly	except
inside	nonsense	kindness	painted
beaches	hopeful	rename	precook

Words With Prefixes

Words With Suffixes

Brainwork! Make four new words from those in the Word Bank. For each new word, take off the suffix or prefix and add a new suffix or prefix.

Name _____

Syllable Study

Remember! When two consonants come between two vowels in a word, the word is usually divided between the two consonants.

Example: sil-ver

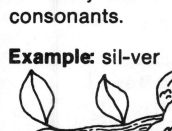

Write each word, dividing it into syllables. Use a hyphen. If a word cannot be divided, circle it.

1. window _____

2. lesson _____

3. butter _____

4. broom _____

5. parrot _____

6. picture _____

7. almost _____

8. number _____

9. happen _____

10. dark _____

11. garden _____

12. monkey _____

13. walnut _____

14. picnic _____

15. winter _____

16. might _____

17. suppose _____

18. doctor _____

19. thirteen _____

20. sister _____

Brainwork! Make a list of all the vowels and another list of all the consonants.

 FS-32031 Reading Activities

Name _____

Syllable Fun

Remember! When three consonants come between two vowels, the word is usually divided between the first two consonants.
Example: sur-prise

Write the word from the Word Box that makes sense in the sentence.

1. His great grandmother lived to be

   a _____ years old.

2. The playground was full of noisy

   _____.

3. The singing telegram was a

   big _____.

Word Box
surprise
hungry
hundred
Pilgrims
children

4. At Thanksgiving I read about the _____.

5. Before breakfast Sue is very _____.

Write the answer words from the sentences above, dividing them into syllables. Use a hyphen.

1. _____   3. _____

2. _____   4. _____

5. _____

Brainwork! Make a list of ten breakfast foods. Write the number of syllables beside each word.

94

Working With Syllables

Write the word that makes sense in the sentence, dividing it into syllables. Use a hyphen.

| doctor | sister | suppose |
| hungry | children | thirteen |

1. Our class has twenty-six _____ .

2. Where do you _____ Kelly is?

3. Dan read _____ books last summer.

4. Are you getting _____ for lunch?

5. Jenny is my older _____ .

6. The _____ gave Mother some medicine.

Check your work. Write each word divided into syllables on the blanks below. Be sure to use a blank for the hyphen, too.
Check: Is every hyphen in the box?

1. _ _ _ _ _ _ _ _ _ _ _ _ _

2. _ _ _ _ _ _ _ _ _ _ _ _ _

3. _ _ _ _ _ _ _ _ _ _ _ _ _

4. _ _ _ _ _ _ _ _ _ _ _ _ _

5. _ _ _ _ _ _ _ _ _ _ _ _ _

6. _ _ _ _ _ _ _ _ _ _ _ _ _

Brainwork! Find the answer words that have three vowels. Write a sentence for each one.

More Syllables

Remember! When one consonant comes between two vowels in a word, and the first vowel is short, the word is usually divided after the consonant.

Example: rĭv-er

Read each sentence. Look at the word in bold type. Mark a ˘ over the first short vowel. Write the word, dividing it into syllables. Use a hyphen.

1. Did you see a **robin** in the nest?   _____

2. Brad is a good **figure** skater.   _____

3. I had some **melon** for lunch.   _____

4. Her pet **lizard** escaped.   _____

5. Put the groceries in the **wagon**.   _____

6. The **lemon** tree is blossoming.   _____

7. Abe grew up in a log **cabin**.   _____

8. My **shadow** looks ten feet tall.   _____

9. Where are the **seven** new books?   _____

10. Look at the **planet** Mars.   _____

Brainwork! On the back of this paper, write two of the above sentences. Then write the number of syllables above each word in the sentence.

Choose a Word

Remember! When one consonant comes between two vowels in a word, and the first vowel is long, the word is usually divided before the consonant.
Example: sō-fa

Write the word that names each picture. Use a hyphen to divide it into syllables. Mark ⎯ over the first vowel if it is long.

1.

ti-ger

2.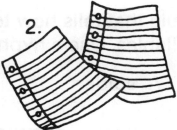

_____

3.

_____

4.

_____

5.

_____

6.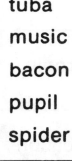

_____

7.

_____

8.

_____

9.

_____

10.

_____

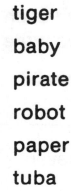

| tiger |
| baby |
| pirate |
| robot |
| paper |
| tuba |
| music |
| bacon |
| pupil |
| spider |

Brainwork! Choose three words from the word list. Write a sentence for each one.

FS-32031 Reading Activities

What's the Rule?

Rule A: When one consonant comes between two vowels in a word, and the first vowel is **short**, the word is usually divided **after** the consonant. **Example:** riv-er

Rule B: When one consonant comes between two vowels in a word, and the first vowel is **long**, the word is usually divided **before** the consonant. **Example:** fu-ture

Read each word. Write **A** or **B** for the rule that tells how to divide it. Then write the word, dividing it into syllables. Use a hyphen.

1. music

____ _____

2. seven

____ _____

3. robin

____ _____

4. bacon

____ _____

5. paper

____ _____

6. second

____ _____

7. spider

____ _____

8. river

____ _____

9. baby

____ _____

10. salad

____ _____

11. china

____ _____

12. silent

____ _____

Brainwork! Choose three words from above. Write a sentence for each one.

Word Choice

Remember! When a vowel is sounded alone in a word, it is a syllable by itself.
Examples: e-rase, dis-a-gree

Write each word below its definition, dividing it into syllables.

| again | open | magazine | Canada | ocean |
| Irish | alive | gasoline | telephone | animals |

1. not closed

   _____

2. one more time

   _____

3. from Ireland

   _____

4. something to talk into

   _____

5. something to read

   _____

6. lions, bears, wolves

   _____

7. a country

   _____

8. fuel for a car

   _____

9. living

   _____

10. a whale's home

    _____

Brainwork! What is your favorite magazine? Write three reasons why it's your favorite.

Thinking About Syllables

Remember! When two vowels are together in a word and have separate sounds, the word is divided between the two vowels.

Example: li-on

Write the word that makes sense in the sentence. Use hyphens to divide the word into syllables.

poem	poet	cruel	giant	diet
science	radio	create	lion	idea

1. Someone who writes a poem is a _____ .

2. Todd has written a _____ .

3. It's about a huge _____ .

4. The giant had a pet _____ .

5. He was kind, not _____ .

6. The giant shrank when he went on a _____ .

7. Where did Todd get the _____ to write?

8. He listened to the _____ .

9. It was fun to _____ a giant.

10. Todd likes writing and _____ , too.

Brainwork! Write a poem about something you learned in science.

FS-32031 Reading Activities

Ending Syllables

Remember! When a word ends in a consonant plus **le,** the word is divided before the consonant. **Example:** pur-ple

Circle the word that has a consonant plus **le** at the end. Write the word, dividing it into syllables. Use a hyphen.

1. Megan can ride in a circle.   _____

2. Her new bike is purple.   _____

3. On the handle is a basket.   _____

4. Megan gives her poodle a ride.   _____

5. People know when she is coming.   _____

6. Megan likes to whistle and ride.   _____

7. It's fun to ride through a puddle.   _____

8. She can watch the water ripple.   _____

9. There is a beetle.   _____

10. Megan stops to rest a little while.   _____

11. She can have an apple.   _____

12. She is able to ride far.   _____

Brainwork! List five more words that end with a consonant plus **le.**

FS-32031 Reading Activities

Rules to Remember

Read each rule. Then write the words, dividing them into syllables.

A. A word with one syllable is never divided.

right _____

block _____

B. A compound word is divided between the two words that make the compound word.

inside _____

sunshine _____

C. When a word has a prefix, the word is divided between the prefix and the base word.

return _____

unclear _____

D. When a word has a suffix, the word is divided between the base word and the suffix.

healthful _____

skating _____

E. When two consonants come between two vowels in a word, the word is usually divided between the two consonants.

winter _____

rubber _____

F. When three consonants come between two vowels, the word is divided between the first two consonants.

surprise _____

children _____

Brainwork! Choose one of the rules above. List five words that follow that rule.

I Know Syllables!

Read each rule. Then write the words, dividing them into syllables.

1. When one consonant comes between two vowels in a word, and the first vowel is short, the word is usually divided after the consonant.

   second _____

   river _____

2. When one consonant comes between two vowels in a word, and the first vowel is long, the word is usually divided before the consonant.

   spider _____

   future _____

3. When a vowel is sounded alone in a word, it is a syllable by itself.

   erase _____

   open _____

4. When two vowels are together in a word and have separate sounds, the word is divided between the two vowels.

   poet _____

   lion _____

5. When a word ends in a consonant plus **le,** the word is divided before the consonant.

   purple _____

   little _____

Brainwork! Choose one of the rules above. Write five words that follow that rule.

FS-32031 Reading Activities

What's Your Syllable Score?

Read each word. Fill in the circle beside the word that is correctly divided into syllables.

1. hundred
O hund-red
O hun-dred
O hundr-ed

2. puddle
O pudd-le
O pud-dle
O puddl-e

3. football
O foot-ball
O footb-all
O fo-otball

4. unwrap
O unwr-ap
O un-wrap
O unw-rap

5. cabin
O ca-bin
O c-abin
O cab-in

6. ocean
O oc-ean
O oce-an
O o-cean

7. poem
O p-oem
O poe-m
O po-em

8. peach
O p-each
O peach
O peac-h

9. robot
O rob-ot
O robo-t
O ro-bot

10. sweetness
O sw-eetness
O sweetn-ess
O sweet-ness

11. picnic
O pic-nic
O pi-cnic
O picnic

My Score:

Answer Key

FS-32031 Reading Activities

Page 1

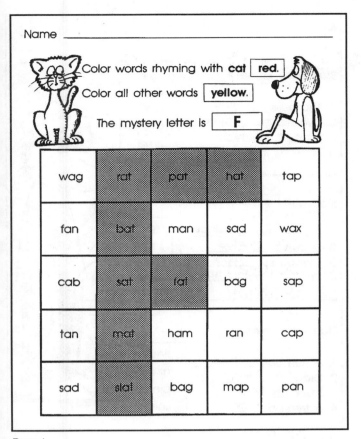

Name _____

Color words rhyming with **cat** red.

Color all other words yellow.

The mystery letter is **F**

wag	rat	pat	hat	tap
fan	bat	man	sad	wax
cab	sat	fat	bag	sap
tan	mat	ham	ran	cap
sad	slat	bag	map	pan

Page 2

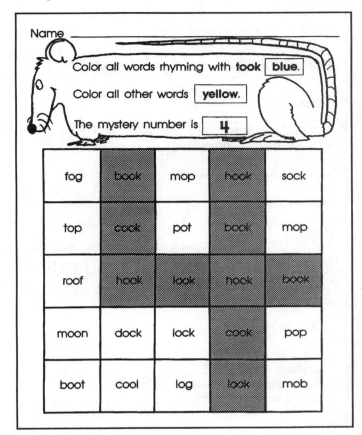

Name _____

Color all words rhyming with **took** blue.

Color all other words yellow.

The mystery number is **4**

fog	book	mop	hook	sock
top	cook	pot	book	mop
roof	hook	took	hook	book
moon	dock	lock	cook	pop
boot	cool	log	look	mob

Page 3

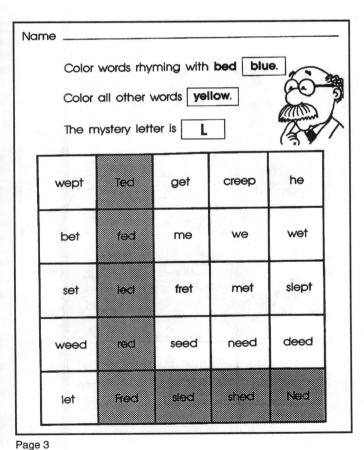

Name _____

Color words rhyming with **bed** blue.

Color all other words yellow.

The mystery letter is **L**

wept	Ted	get	creep	he
bet	fed	me	we	wet
set	led	fret	met	slept
weed	red	seed	need	deed
let	fred	sled	shed	Ned

Page 4

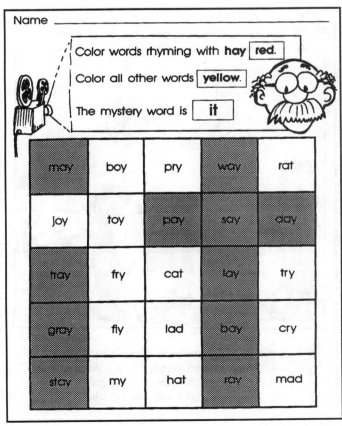

Name _____

Color words rhyming with **hay** red.

Color all other words yellow.

The mystery word is **it**

may	boy	pry	way	rat
joy	toy	pay	say	day
tray	fry	cat	lay	try
gray	fly	lad	bay	cry
stay	my	hat	ray	mad

Answer Key

Name _____

Start with rate.

1. Don't be ___late___ .
2. Close the ___gate___ .
3. Eat a ___date___ .
4. To **not** like: ___hate___

hate	
late	
date	
gate	

_____

Start with pain.

1. A spot: ___stain___
2. To add weight: ___gain___
3. From the clouds: ___rain___
4. Choo, choo ___train___

train	
rain	
stain	
gain	

_____

Start with ray.

1. Know your ___way___ .
2. Monday is a ___day___ .
3. Black and white make ___gray___ .
4. To put down: ___lay___

lay	
gray	
day	
way	

Page 5

Name _____

Start with crime.

1. The bells ___chime___ .
2. Two nickels: ___dime___
3. Clock: ___time___
4. A green fruit: ___lime___

dime	
lime	
chime	
time	

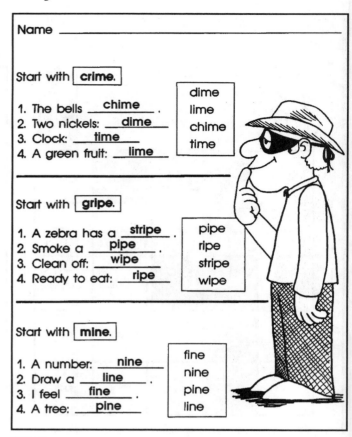

_____

Start with gripe.

1. A zebra has a ___stripe___ .
2. Smoke a ___pipe___ .
3. Clean off: ___wipe___
4. Ready to eat: ___ripe___

pipe	
ripe	
stripe	
wipe	

_____

Start with mine.

1. A number: ___nine___
2. Draw a ___line___ .
3. I feel ___fine___ .
4. A tree: ___pine___

fine	
nine	
pine	
line	

Page 6

Name _____

If it rhymes with **man**, color it **red**.
If it rhymes with **noon**, color it **yellow**.
If it rhymes with **rock**, color it **green**.
If it rhymes with **float**, color it **blue**.

Page 7

Name _____

If it rhymes with **mail**, put a **red dot** on it.

If it rhymes with **bar**, mark it with **green**.

If it rhymes with **see**, make a **yellow X** on it.

Page 8

Answer Key

If it rhymes with **ring**, color it **red**.
If it rhymes with **big**, color it **yellow**.
If it rhymes with **wet**, color it **blue**.
If it rhymes with **Ben**, color it **green**.

Page 9

Name _____ Skill: Compound Words

Directions: Paste a [boat] to [sail].
Make a new word.
Write the compound word.

rattle	snake	rattlesnake
base	ball	baseball
mail	man	mailman
pan	cakes	pancakes
flag	pole	flagpole

ball   cakes   snake   pole   man

Page 10

Name _____ Skill: Compound Words

Directions: Make a compound word from 2 words.
Write the word.

1. flag + pole
   flagpole
2. base + ball
   baseball
3. dog + house
   doghouse
4. butter + fly
   butterfly
5. hair + brush
   hairbrush
6. lady + bug
   ladybug
7. bare + foot
   barefoot
8. shoe + lace
   shoelace
9. play + pen
   playpen
10. cup + cake
    cupcake

Page 11

Name _____ Skill: Compound Words

Directions: Write the two words that make up each compound word.

blueberry	blue	berry
popcorn	pop	corn
football	foot	ball
downstairs	down	stairs
sidewalk	side	walk
raincoat	rain	coat
outside	out	side

beehive	bee	hive
snowstorm	snow	storm
cowboy	cow	boy

Page 12

107

FS-32031 Reading Activities

Answer Key

Name _____ Skill: Compound Words

Directions: Write the missing compound word in each sentence.

| sunshine | anyone | fireman | myself | baseball |
| pancakes | birthday | afternoon | doorbell | airplane |

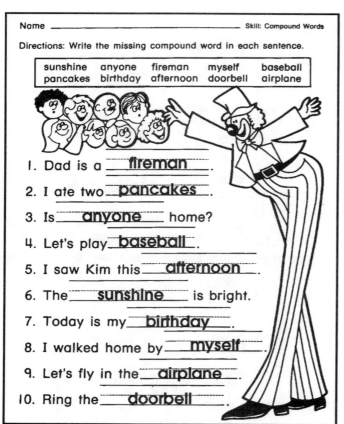

1. Dad is a __fireman__.
2. I ate two __pancakes__.
3. Is __anyone__ home?
4. Let's play __baseball__.
5. I saw Kim this __afternoon__.
6. The __sunshine__ is bright.
7. Today is my __birthday__.
8. I walked home by __myself__.
9. Let's fly in the __airplane__.
10. Ring the __doorbell__.

Page 13

Name _____ Skill: Compound Words

Directions: Find a word to go with each meaning.

| bookcase | driveway | shoelace | cupboard | doorbell |
| bathtub | mailbox | bedroom | classroom | doorknob |

1. a place for letters __mailbox__
2. a place to sleep __bedroom__
3. for tying shoes __shoelace__
4. a place for books __bookcase__
5. for taking a bath __bathtub__
6. a place to learn __classroom__
7. use to open door __doorknob__
8. place for dishes __cupboard__
9. place for the car __driveway__
10. tells you someone is at the door __doorbell__

Page 14

Name _____ Skill: Compound words

Compound Word Splits

Place the given letters in each grid to form a compound word.
The words go across, then down. Use the pictures below as clues.

Write the completed compound word beside the correct picture.

1. pieo

| t | i | p |
| o |
| e |

2. aupke

| c | u | p |
| a |
| k |
| e |

3. hinnue

| s | u | n |
| h |
| i |
| n |
| e |

4. eciphap

| s | p | a | c | e |
| h |
| i |
| p |

5. htirda

| b | i | r | d |
| a |
| t |
| h |

6. ropee

| t | r | e | e |
| o |
| p |

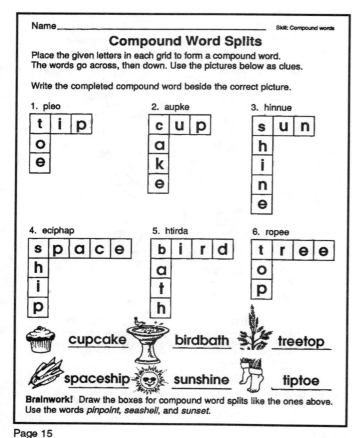

cupcake   birdbath   treetop
spaceship   sunshine   tiptoe

Brainwork! Draw the boxes for compound word splits like the ones above. Use the words *pinpoint*, *seashell*, and *sunset*.

Page 15

Name _____ Skill: Compound words

Compound Word Splits

Place the given letters in each grid to form a compound word.
The words go down, then across. Use the pictures below as clues.

Write the completed compound word beside the correct picture.

1. tcot

	c
o	u	t
	t

2. ekpnc

	p
c	a	k	e
	n

3. llshde

	h
s	i	d	e
	l
	l

4. whkrme

| h |
| w | o | r | k |
| m |
| e |

5. llwtref

	w
f	a	l	l
	t
	e
	r

6. bblsel

	b
b	a	l	l
	s
	e

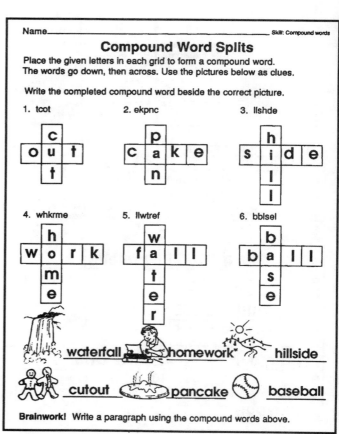

waterfall   homework   hillside
cutout   pancake   baseball

Brainwork! Write a paragraph using the compound words above.

Page 16

108

Answer Key

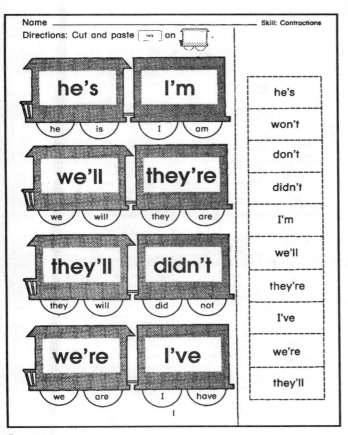

Directions: Cut and paste [____] on [____].

Skill: Contractions

he's	I'm
he is	I am

we'll	they're
we will	they are

they'll	didn't
they will	did not

we're	I've
we are	I have

he's
won't
don't
didn't
I'm
we'll
they're
I've
we're
they'll

Page 17

Name _____ Skill: Contractions
Directions: Write a contraction for the 2 words in ( ).

1. __I'll__ be home soon.
   (I will)

2. Jan __won't__ play.
   (will not)

3. We __aren't__ ready.
   (are not)

4. That __isn't__ my hat.
   (is not)

5. I think __she'll__ cry.
   (she will)

6. Tod __didn't__ find the cat.
   (did not)

7. __You'll__ like that book.
   (You will)

8. Hurry or __we'll__ be late.
   (we will)

9. Kim __doesn't__ live here.
   (does not)

10. __They'll__ ring the bell.
    (they will)

(she'll, we'll, I'll, they'll, you'll, will)
(aren't, didn't, isn't, doesn't, won't)

Page 18

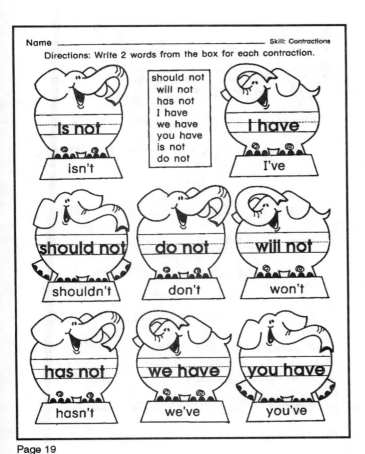

Name _____ Skill: Contractions
Directions: Write 2 words from the box for each contraction.

should not
will not
has not
I have
we have
you have
is not
do not

is not	I have
isn't	I've

should not	do not	will not
shouldn't	don't	won't

has not	we have	you have
hasn't	we've	you've

Page 19

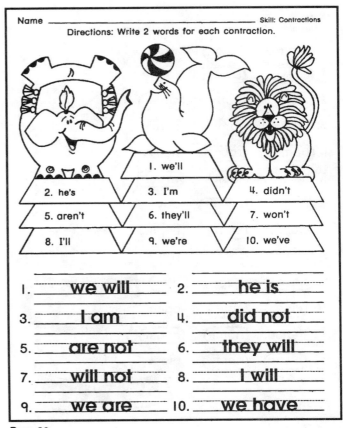

Name _____ Skill: Contractions
Directions: Write 2 words for each contraction.

1. we'll		
2. he's	3. I'm	4. didn't
5. aren't	6. they'll	7. won't
8. I'll	9. we're	10. we've

1. __we will__ 2. __he is__
3. __I am__ 4. __did not__
5. __are not__ 6. __they will__
7. __will not__ 8. __I will__
9. __we are__ 10. __we have__

Page 20

109

FS-32031 Reading Activities

Answer Key

Page 21

Name _____ Skill: Contractions

Directions: Write contractions. Cross out letters you do not use.

1. we are **we're**
2. could not **couldn't**
3. he is **he's**
4. they will **they'll**
5. I am **I'm**
6. we have **we've**
7. she will **she'll**
8. cannot **can't**
9. did not **didn't**
10. do not **don't**
11. she is **she's**
12. they are **they're**

Page 21

Page 22

Name _____ Skill: Synonyms

Directions: Write a word from the box that has the same meaning.

pan	yell	house	glue	rip	bag
dish	gift	cry	sick	cup	smile

shout **yell**	plate **dish**
home **house**	present **gift**
grin **smile**	weep **cry**
paste **glue**	tear **rip**
ill **sick**	mug **cup**
pot **pan**	sack **bag**

Page 22

Page 23

Name _____ Skill: Synonyms

Directions: Circle two words that have almost the same meaning.

(large) (big) thin

1. (easy) (simple) funny
2. (tiny) baby (small)
3. dance (jump) (leap)
4. (bumpy) (rough) heavy
5. hear (look) (watch)
6. (fix) (repair) buy
7. stop (start) (begin)
8. (quick) (fast) run
9. (smile) happy (grin)
10. (close) (shut) open
11. fence (home) (house)
12. (mean) (nasty) big

Page 23

Page 24

Name _____ Skill: Synonyms

Directions: Write a word that has almost the same meaning as the underlined word.

like	silly	watch	yell	unhappy
fuzzy	largest	turn	scared	leaped

1. I enjoy watching the clowns. **like**
2. The sad clown is the best. **unhappy**
3. He is riding the biggest bike. **largest**
4. Watch the bike spin around. **turn**
5. Here comes the furry dog. **fuzzy**
6. He looks funny in a clown's hat. **silly**
7. Did you see the dog jump? **watch**
8. It jumped into the basket. **leaped**
9. Is the dog frightened? **scared**
10. Let's clap and shout for the dog! **yell**

Page 24

FS-32031 Reading Activities

Answer Key

Take My Place

Skill: Synonyms

Choose the word from the Word Box that could take the place of the boldfaced word in each sentence. Write it on the line.

Word Box

thick   whole   help   choose   careful   piece

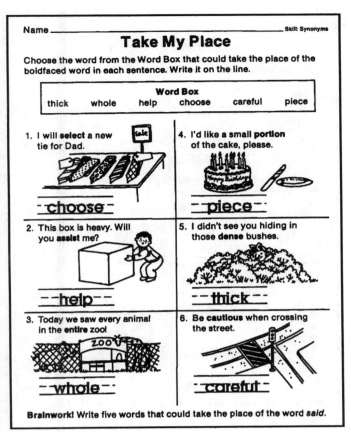

1. I will **select** a new tie for Dad.
choose

4. I'd like a small **portion** of the cake, please.
piece

2. This box is heavy. Will you **assist** me?
help

5. I didn't see you hiding in those **dense** bushes.
thick

3. Today we saw every animal in the **entire** zoo!
whole

6. Be **cautious** when crossing the street.
careful

Brainwork! Write five words that could take the place of the word *said*.

Page 25

Figure It Out

Skill: Synonyms

Read each sentence. Use the picture clue to help you figure out the meaning of the boldfaced word. Circle the correct meaning. Write it on the line.

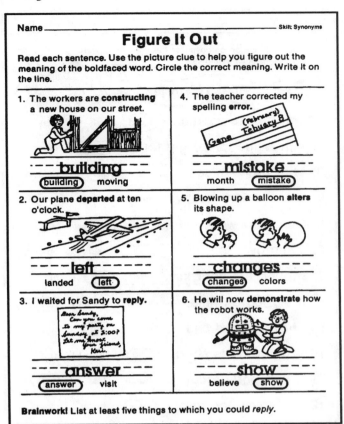

1. The workers are **constructing** a new house on our street.
building
(building)   moving

4. The teacher corrected my spelling **error**.
mistake
month   (mistake)

2. Our plane **departed** at ten o'clock.
left
landed   (left)

5. Blowing up a balloon **alters** its shape.
changes
(changes)   colors

3. I waited for Sandy to **reply**.
answer
(answer)   visit

6. He will now **demonstrate** how the robot works.
show
believe   (show)

Brainwork! List at least five things to which you could *reply*.

Page 26

Skill: Antonyms

Directions: Find a word that means the opposite. Write the number of the antonym.

1. right	2. sun	3. laugh	4. dirty
5. day	6. big	7. sad	8. break
9. full	10. over	11. float	12. open

2 moon   8 fix
7 happy   11 sink
9 empty   1 left
4 clean   5 night
3 cry   12 closed
6 small   10 under

Page 27

Skill: Antonyms

Directions: Write an antonym for the word in the ▢ for each sentence.

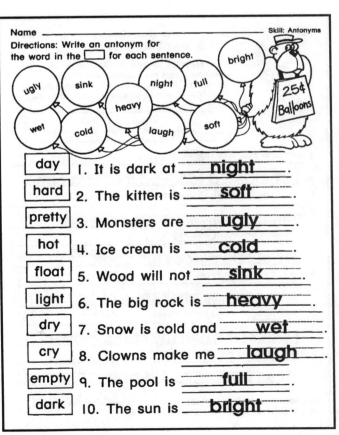

ugly   sink   night   full   bright
wet   cold   heavy   laugh   soft

day   1. It is dark at **night**.
hard   2. The kitten is **soft**.
pretty 3. Monsters are **ugly**.
hot   4. Ice cream is **cold**.
float 5. Wood will not **sink**.
light 6. The big rock is **heavy**.
dry   7. Snow is cold and **wet**.
cry   8. Clowns make me **laugh**.
empty 9. The pool is **full**.
dark   10. The sun is **bright**.

Page 28

Answer Key

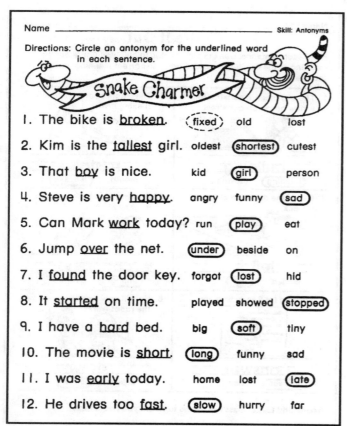

Name _____ Skill: Antonyms

Directions: Circle an antonym for the underlined word in each sentence.

Snake Charmer

1. The bike is <u>broken</u>. (fixed) old lost
2. Kim is the <u>tallest</u> girl. oldest (shortest) cutest
3. That <u>boy</u> is nice. kid (girl) person
4. Steve is very <u>happy</u>. angry funny (sad)
5. Can Mark <u>work</u> today? run (play) eat
6. Jump <u>over</u> the net. (under) beside on
7. I <u>found</u> the door key. forgot (lost) hid
8. It <u>started</u> on time. played showed (stopped)
9. I have a <u>hard</u> bed. big (soft) tiny
10. The movie is <u>short</u>. (long) funny sad
11. I was <u>early</u> today. home lost (late)
12. He drives too <u>fast</u>. (slow) hurry far

Page 29

Name _____ Skill: Antonyms

Get the Picture

Look at each picture and sentence. One word in the sentence is wrong. Circle the wrong word. Then write the word that would make the sentence true.

1. Pam is surprised because there is (something) in the box.
   __nothing__
   nothing everything

2. The plane will (leave) at one o'clock.
   __arrive__
   runway arrive

3. Tim doesn't know that there is a bee on the (front) of his shirt.
   __back__
   sleeve back

4. When you set the table, place the fork on the (right) side of the plate.
   __left__
   left same

5. Kim is (sad) because she found the missing bunny.
   __happy__
   tired happy

6. He stayed in bed because he was (well).
   __sick__
   sick young

Brainwork! The words *never* and *always* are opposites. Make a safety poster which has an "always" and a "never" rule.

Page 30

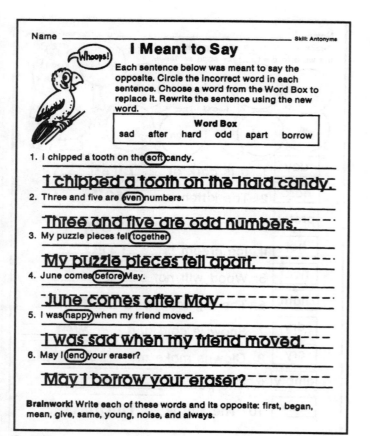

Name _____ Skill: Antonyms

I Meant to Say

Whoops!

Each sentence below was meant to say the opposite. Circle the incorrect word in each sentence. Choose a word from the Word Box to replace it. Rewrite the sentence using the new word.

Word Box
sad after hard odd apart borrow

1. I chipped a tooth on the (soft) candy.
   I chipped a tooth on the hard candy.
2. Three and five are (even) numbers.
   Three and five are odd numbers.
3. My puzzle pieces fell (together).
   My puzzle pieces fell apart.
4. June comes (before) May.
   June comes after May.
5. I was (happy) when my friend moved.
   I was sad when my friend moved.
6. May I (lend) your eraser?
   May I borrow your eraser?

Brainwork! Write each of these words and its opposite: first, began, mean, give, same, young, noise, and always.

Page 31

Name _____ Skill: Synonyms/Antonyms

Directions: Use a word from the box to write a synonym or antonym for each word.

tardy	sad	jolly	big	frown	lower	yellow
fat	thin	quiet	lift	close	loud	break
mend	far	grin	stop	early	small	start

1. (antonym) happy **sad**
2. (synonym) fix **mend**
3. (synonym) noisy **loud**
4. (antonym) raise **lower**
5. (synonym) near **close**
6. (antonym) smile **frown**
7. (antonym) fat **thin**
8. (synonym) large **big**
9. (antonym) late **early**
10. (synonym) begin **start**

Page 32

FS-32031 Reading Activities

Answer Key

Name _____ Skill: Homonyms

Directions: Write the correct missing word on the line.

1. My **son** Ted is six.

2. I **ate** a hot dog.

3. **I** lost my key.

4. Comb your **hair**.

5. I hurt my **right** arm.

6. Pick a **flower**.

7. I went last **night**.

8. I **see** a baby bird.

9. My dog eats **meat**.

10. Let's **sail** the boat.

Page 33

Name _____ Skill: Homonyms

Directions: Match the words that sound the same. Write the number beside the word it matches.

1. right 2. bear 3. dear 4. eight

5. cent 6. sea 7. I 8. flour

9. pear 10. so 11. blew 12. ring

---

7 eye 1 write 10 sew 9 pair

12 wring 3 deer 2 bare 8 flower

11 blue 6 see 4 ate 5 scent

Page 34

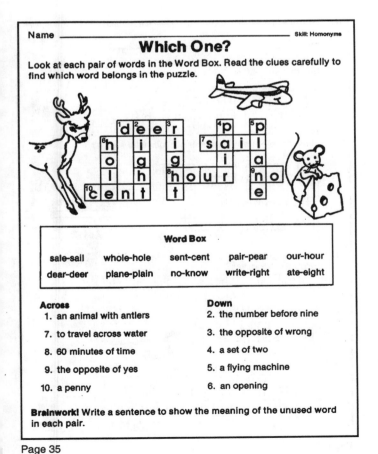

Name _____ Skill: Homonyms

Which One?

Look at each pair of words in the Word Box. Read the clues carefully to find which word belongs in the puzzle.

Word Box

sale-sail	whole-hole	sent-cent	pair-pear	our-hour
dear-deer	plane-plain	no-know	write-right	ate-eight

Across
1. an animal with antlers
7. to travel across water
8. 60 minutes of time
9. the opposite of yes
10. a penny

Down
2. the number before nine
3. the opposite of wrong
4. a set of two
5. a flying machine
6. an opening

Brainwork! Write a sentence to show the meaning of the unused word in each pair.

Page 35

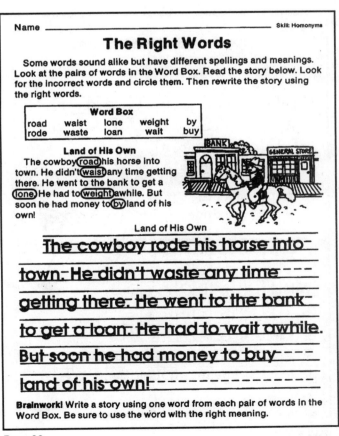

Name _____ Skill: Homonyms

The Right Words

Some words sound alike but have different spellings and meanings. Look at the pairs of words in the Word Box. Read the story below. Look for the incorrect words and circle them. Then rewrite the story using the right words.

Word Box

road	waist	lone	weight	by
rode	waste	loan	wait	buy

Land of His Own

The cowboy (road) his horse into town. He didn't (waist) any time getting there. He went to the bank to get a (lone). He had to (weight) awhile. But soon he had money to (by) land of his own!

Land of His Own

The cowboy rode his horse into town. He didn't waste any time getting there. He went to the bank to get a loan. He had to wait awhile. But soon he had money to buy land of his own!

Brainwork! Write a story using one word from each pair of words in the Word Box. Be sure to use the word with the right meaning.

Page 36

113

FS-32031 Reading Activities

Answer Key

Page 37

Name _____

Write the letter that comes **before** the letter in the box. Put it **above** to find the answer to the riddle.

1. Which American president wore the largest hat?

The	one	with	the
uif	pof	xjui	uif

largest	head	.
mbshftu	ifbe	

2. Life is tough . . . but what can you always count on?

your	fingers
zpvs	gjohfst

3. What animal can fly higher than a house?

all	of	them	—
bmm	pg	uifn	

houses	can't	fly
ipvtft	dbou	gmz

4. What time is it when a clock strikes 13?

time	to	get	a
ujnf	up	hfu	b

new	clock
ofx	dmpdl

5. What is the oldest piece of furniture in the world?

the	multiplication	table
uif	nvmujqmjdbujpo	ubcmf

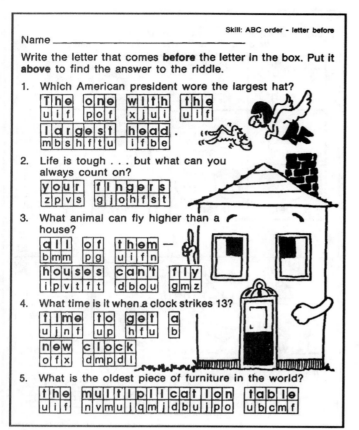

Page 38

Name _____

Write the letter that comes after the letter in the box. Put it below to find the answer to the riddle.

1. What is the best way to keep goats from smelling?

bts	nee	sgdhq	mnrdr
Cut	off	their	noses

2. What is the worst weather for rats and mice?

vgdm	hs	q	hmr	b	sr	mc
when	it	rains	cats	and

cnfr
dogs

3. Why do monsters like to live in dark places?

vgn	jmnvr	sg	sr	sgd
Who	knows?	That's	the

v	x	lnmrsdqr	qd
Way	monsters	are.

4. What is gray?

	ldksdc	odmfthm
a	melted	penguin

5. What is red and round and goes putt putt?

m	ntsan	qc	ookd
an	outboard	apple

RESIDENCE OF V. SCARY MONSTER, ESQ.

Page 39

Name _____

Secret Alphabet Messages

Find the secret message.

Under each letter, write the letter that comes next in the alphabet.

Q D Z C H M F	O T Y Y K D R
R E A D I N G	P U Z Z L E S

Z M C	F Z L D R
A N D	G A M E S

Z Q D	E T M
A R E	F U N .

Under each letter, write the letter that comes before it in the alphabet.

X I J D I	E P	Z P V
W H I C H	D O	Y O U

M J L F	C F U U F S
L I K E	B E T T E R —

S F B E J O H	P S	N B U I
R E A D I N G	O R	M A T H ?

Brainwork! Create a different alphabet code. Write a short message and directions for decoding it. Give it to a friend to decode.

Page 40

Name _____

Write the letter that comes **between** the letter above and below to find the answer to the riddle.

1. Why did the giraffe stand on his head?

sn	sqho	btqhntr	ahqcr
to	trip	curious	birds
up	usjiq	dvsjpvt	cjset

2. Why do elephants paint their toenails purple?

rn	sgdx	b m	ghcd
so	they	can	hide
tp	uifz	dbo	ijef

hm	fq od	uhmdr
in	grape	vines
jo	hsbqf	wjoft

3. What is green and brown and crawls through the grass?

	fhqk	rbnts	vgn	cqnoodc
a	girl	scout	who	dropped
b	hjsm	tdpvu	xip	espqqfe

gdq	bnnjhd
her	cookie
ifs	dppljf

4. What has a brown jacket and goes 120 miles per hour?

	etdk	hmidbsdc	ons	sn
a	fuel	injected	pota	to
b	gvfm	jokfdufe	qpub	up

FS-32031 Reading Activities

Answer Key

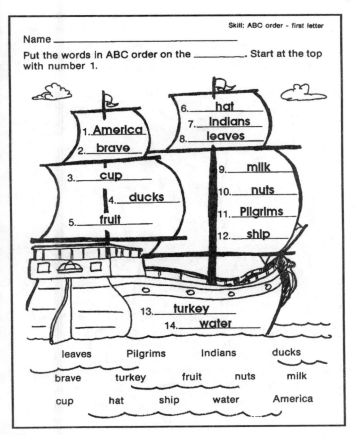

Skill: ABC order - first letter

Name _____

Put the words in ABC order on the _____. Start at the top with number 1.

1. America
2. brave
3. cup
4. ducks
5. fruit
6. hat
7. Indians
8. leaves
9. milk
10. nuts
11. Pilgrims
12. ship
13. turkey
14. water

leaves   Pilgrims   Indians   ducks

brave   turkey   fruit   nuts   milk

cup   hat   ship   water   America

Page 41

Skill: ABC order - first letter

Name _____

Put the words in ABC order on the _____. Start at the top with number 1.

1. ant
2. bear
3. cat   9. kangaroo
4. dog   10. mouse
5. elephant   11. rat
6. fish   12. snake
7. goat   13. turtle
8. hippo   14. zebra

cat   mouse   snake   goat
hippo   rat   fish   dog

zebra   ant   elephant
bear   kangaroo   turtle

Page 42

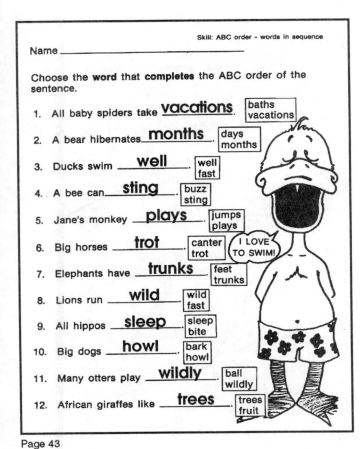

Skill: ABC order - words in sequence

Name _____

Choose the **word** that **completes** the ABC order of the sentence.

1. All baby spiders take **vacations**.   [baths / vacations]
2. A bear hibernates **months**.   [days / months]
3. Ducks swim **well**.   [well / fast]
4. A bee can **sting**.   [buzz / sting]
5. Jane's monkey **plays**.   [jumps / plays]
6. Big horses **trot**.   [canter / trot]   I LOVE TO SWIM!
7. Elephants have **trunks**.   [feet / trunks]
8. Lions run **wild**.   [wild / fast]
9. All hippos **sleep**.   [sleep / bite]
10. Big dogs **howl**.   [bark / howl]
11. Many otters play **wildly**.   [ball / wildly]
12. African giraffes like **trees**.   [trees / fruit]

Page 43

© Frank Schaffer Publications, Inc.

Skill: ABC order - first letter - Tic-Tac-Toe

Name _____

Draw a line through the row in ABC order.
You may go ➡ ⬇ or ↘.

bean	apple	you
zebra	bread	up
dog	cake	ant

desk	train	send
red	fish	are
good	cat	lion

see	take	red
flap	try	ask
Nan	bee	zoo

run	me	see
go	jump	push
find	down	look

two	some	violin
wild	very	corn
one	zebra	eat

sing	you	take
watch	yes	zing
box	toe	swing

Page 44

115

FS-32031 Reading Activities

Answer Key

© Frank Schaffer Publications, Inc.

116

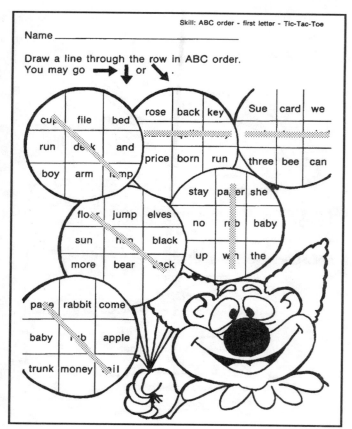

Name _____

Draw a line through the row in ABC order.
You may go ➡ ⬇ or ↘ .

Page 45

Name _____

Find the word that is **out of order** in each numbered picture.
Write **that word** in the **same numbered** blank at the bottom to
find the mystery sentence.

1	2
we	lose
down	men
every	picked
he	now
lion	owl

3	4	5
umbrella	blue	cross
witch	orange	garden
youth	red	hippo
zoom	yellow	flowers
the	purple	line

1 We   2 picked   3 the   4 purple   5 flowers.

Page 46

Name _____

Find the word that is **out of order** in each numbered picture.
Write **that word** in the **same numbered** blank at the bottom to
find the mystery sentence.

1	2	3
apple	take	angry
dogs	violet	down
fire	word	very
gold	yellow	elephant
cats	have	four

4	5
bear	paper
candy	quiz
soft	rat
help	two
ice	fur

1 Cats   2 have   3 very   4 soft   5 fur

Page 47

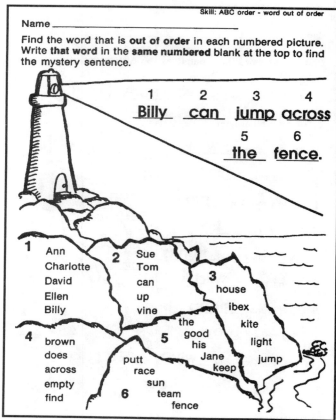

Name _____

Find the word that is **out of order** in each numbered picture.
Write **that word** in the **same numbered** blank at the top to find
the mystery sentence.

1 Billy   2 can   3 jump   4 across
5 the   6 fence.

1	2	3
Ann	Sue	house
Charlotte	Tom	ibex
David	can	kite
Ellen	up	light
Billy	vine	jump

4	5	6
brown	the	putt
does	good	race
across	his	sun
empty	Jane	team
find	keep	fence

Page 48

Answer Key

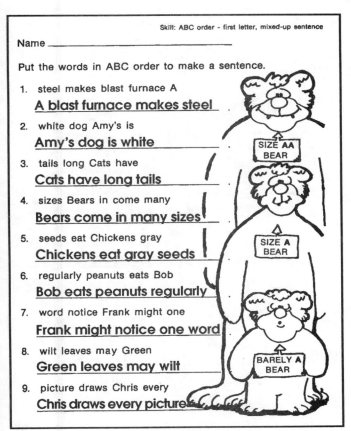

Skill: ABC order - first letter, mixed-up sentence

Name _____

Put the words in ABC order to make a sentence.

1. steel makes blast furnace A
   A blast furnace makes steel

2. white dog Amy's is
   Amy's dog is white

3. tails long Cats have
   Cats have long tails

4. sizes Bears in come many
   Bears come in many sizes

5. seeds eat Chickens gray
   Chickens eat gray seeds

6. regularly peanuts eats Bob
   Bob eats peanuts regularly

7. word notice Frank might one
   Frank might notice one word

8. wilt leaves may Green
   Green leaves may wilt

9. picture draws Chris every
   Chris draws every picture

Page 49

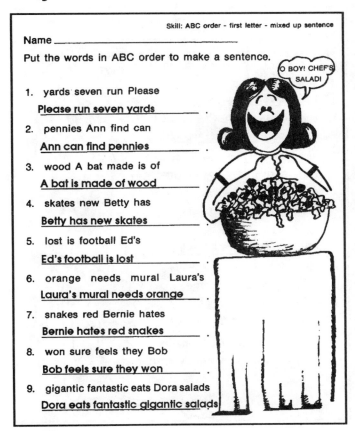

Skill: ABC order - first letter - mixed up sentence

Name _____

Put the words in ABC order to make a sentence.

1. yards seven run Please
   Please run seven yards

2. pennies Ann find can
   Ann can find pennies

3. wood A bat made is of
   A bat is made of wood

4. skates new Betty has
   Betty has new skates

5. lost is football Ed's
   Ed's football is lost

6. orange needs mural Laura's
   Laura's mural needs orange

7. snakes red Bernie hates
   Bernie hates red snakes

8. won sure feels they Bob
   Bob feels sure they won

9. gigantic fantastic eats Dora salads
   Dora eats fantastic gigantic salads

O BOY! CHEF'S SALAD!

Page 50

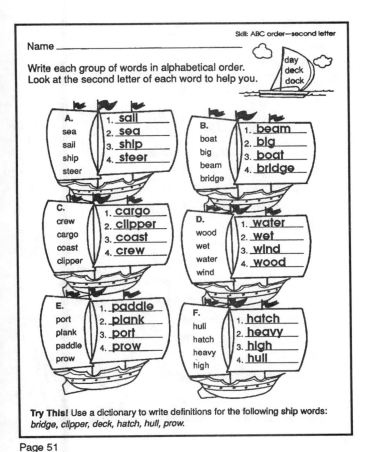

Skill: ABC order—second letter

Name _____

Write each group of words in alphabetical order.
Look at the second letter of each word to help you.

day
deck
dock

A.
sea
sail
ship
steer
1. **sail**
2. **sea**
3. **ship**
4. **steer**

B.
boat
big
beam
bridge
1. **beam**
2. **big**
3. **boat**
4. **bridge**

C.
crew
cargo
coast
clipper
1. **cargo**
2. **clipper**
3. **coast**
4. **crew**

D.
wood
wet
water
wind
1. **water**
2. **wet**
3. **wind**
4. **wood**

E.
port
plank
paddle
prow
1. **paddle**
2. **plank**
3. **port**
4. **prow**

F.
hull
hatch
heavy
high
1. **hatch**
2. **heavy**
3. **high**
4. **hull**

Try This! Use a dictionary to write definitions for the following ship words:
bridge, clipper, deck, hatch, hull, prow.

Page 51

Skill: ABC order - words in sequence - second letter

Name _____

On this page both words complete the ABC order of the sentence. Look at the second letter to choose which word comes first.

1. John's music sounds very **western**   [wrong / western]

2. Ballet can cramp the **toes**   [tummy / toes]

3. Joy sang **softly**   [sweetly / softly]

4. I play the **trumpet**   [tuba / trumpet]

5. Bill is **neat**   [noisy / neat]

6. Alice danced **slowly**   [slowly / swiftly]

7. He sings **songs**   [songs / Sunday]

8. Speed up **Valerie**   [Valerie / Virginia]

9. Hop, skip, **trip**   [trip / tumble]

10. I like to **waltz**   [waltz / wiggle]

11. Betty's flute is **new**   [new / nice]

12. Al's band makes **money**   [music / money]

OOCH OUCH EECH ORCH!

Page 52

FS-32031 Reading Activities

Answer Key

Page 53

Name _____

Put the words in ABC order to make a sentence. Look at the second letter if two words start the same.

1. silver I skies see
   I see silver skies .

2. caught Bob crawfish Louisiana in
   Bob caught crawfish in Louisiana .

3. monsters How many watches own?
   How many monsters own watches ?

4. washing is windows Ira
   Ira is washing windows .

5. roses red My terrific smell
   My red roses smell terrific .

6. sleepy A snail wakes sometimes
   A sleepy snail sometimes wakes .

7. ten Joe tapped turtles tiny
   Joe tapped ten tiny turtles .

8. Lucy mellow Lazy music makes
   Lazy Lucy makes mellow music.

IT'S TIME TO SCARE PEOPLE

Page 53

Page 54

Name _____

Draw a line through the row in ABC order. You may go → ↓ or ↘

sad	step	speech
so	set	sip
sit	sun	soap

be	buy	bow
big	bag	best
bug	bring	but

help	hide	hug
hurt	hat	horse
hinge	hard	him

mine	my	mud
mush	mail	milk
me	mitt	mug

rub	rush	risk
rat	red	rule
rung	rag	read

lap	look	leaf
limp	love	lab
let	lag	lump

Page 54

Page 55

Name _____

Put the words in ABC order on the _____ . Look at the second and third letters if the words start the same. Start with number 1.

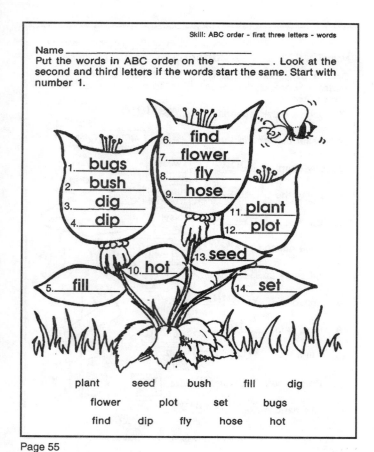

1. bugs
2. bush
3. dig
4. dip
5. fill
6. find
7. flower
8. fly
9. hose
10. hot
11. plant
12. plot
13. seed
14. set

plant   seed   bush   fill   dig
flower   plot   set   bugs
find   dip   fly   hose   hot

Page 55

Page 56

Name _____

Put the words in ABC order to make a sentence. Look at the second and third letters if two words start the same.

1. Harold's handle hat Bob can
   Bob can handle Harold's hat .

2. cashed money Captain his Carl
   Captain Carl cashed his money .

3. bent Amy Betty's big buckle
   Amy bent Betty's big buckle .

4. lets Lew Larry lose
   Larry lets Lew lose .

5. the waiters Ted Tiger tips
   Ted the Tiger tips waiters .

6. Harold Can Hastings smash spiders?
   Can Harold Hastings smash spiders ?

7. Amy mother make Mary mind can
   Amy can make Mary mind mother .

8. television Ted's yellow turned
   Ted's television turned yellow .

9. on is glue Gloria's glad Be not you
   Be glad Gloria's glue is not on you .

Page 56

118

Answer Key

Go-Togethers

Look at each group of words below. First cross out the word that does not belong. Then add a word from the Word Box that does belong.

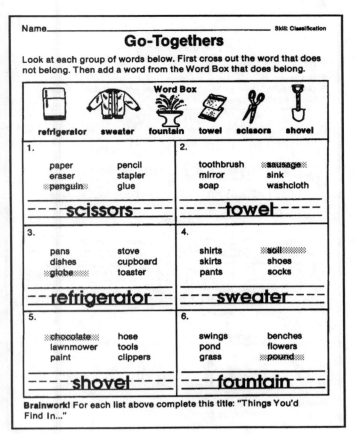

Word Box

refrigerator   sweater   fountain   towel   scissors   shovel

1.
paper   pencil
eraser   stapler
~~penguin~~ glue

__scissors__

2.
toothbrush   ~~sausage~~
mirror   sink
soap   washcloth

__towel__

3.
pans   stove
dishes   cupboard
~~globe~~   toaster

__refrigerator__

4.
shirts   ~~soil~~
skirts   shoes
pants   socks

__sweater__

5.
~~chocolate~~ hose
lawnmower   tools
paint   clippers

__shovel__

6.
swings   benches
pond   flowers
grass   ~~pound~~

__fountain__

Brainwork! For each list above complete this title: "Things You'd Find In..."

Page 57

Whirl-a-Word Puzzles

The puzzles below contain the names of four instruments used for seeing. Follow the directions to discover the name of each instrument.

Begin at the ★. Count every two letters and circle the letter. Then write the circled letters in the correct order on the blanks below the puzzle.

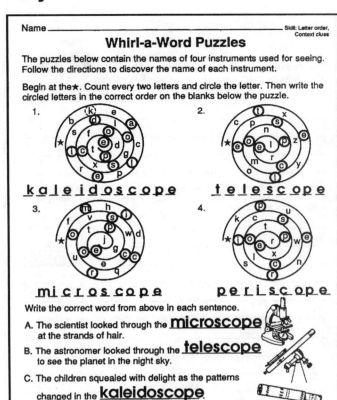

1. __k a l e i d o s c o p e__

2. __t e l e s c o p e__

3. __m i c r o s c o p e__

4. __p e r i s c o p e__

Write the correct word from above in each sentence.

A. The scientist looked through the **microscope** at the strands of hair.

B. The astronomer looked through the **telescope** to see the planet in the night sky.

C. The children squealed with delight as the patterns changed in the **kaleidoscope**.

Brainwork! Create a whirl-a-word puzzle using a word 10 to 12 letters long.

Page 58

Kaleidoscope Fun

Rearrange the letters in each circle to make two or three words. Write the letters in the boxes below the circle.

t e a
a t e (eat)

b a g
g a b

r e a d
d e a r

s t o p   (tops,
s p o t   pots,
           post)

s l a p   (laps)
p a l s

s t e p
p e t s
p e s t

s n a p
p a n s
n a p s

Brainwork! Some words are spelled the same forward and backward like the word *mom*. Think of three more words like this. Write them.

Page 59

Kaleidoscope Game

Rearrange the letters in each circle to make two or three words. Write the letters in the boxes below the circle.

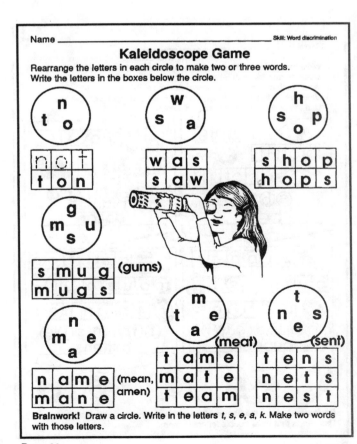

n o t
t o n

w a s
s a w

s h o p
h o p s

s m u g   (gums)
m u g s

n a m e   (mean,
m a n e   amen)

t a m e   (meat)
m a t e
t e a m

t e n s   (sent)
n e t s
n e s t

Brainwork! Draw a circle. Write in the letters *t, s, e, a, k.* Make two words with those letters.

Page 60

119

Answer Key

Name Puzzle

Answers vary Skill: Generating words

Write your **first** name in the boxes below. Write one letter to a box. If there's room, write your **middle** name. Then make as many words from these letters as you can.

☐ ☐ ☐ ☐ ☐ ☐ ☐ ☐ ☐ ☐ ☐ ☐ ☐ ☐

_____   _____

_____   _____

_____   _____

Write your **last** name in the boxes below. Write one letter to a box. If there's room, write your **middle** name. Then make as many words from these letters as you can.

☐ ☐ ☐ ☐ ☐ ☐ ☐ ☐ ☐ ☐ ☐ ☐ ☐ ☐

_____   _____

_____   _____

_____   _____

Write three sentences using at least four of the words you made above.

_____

_____

_____

Brainwork! Make another name puzzle like the one above. Use the name of someone in your school.

Page 61

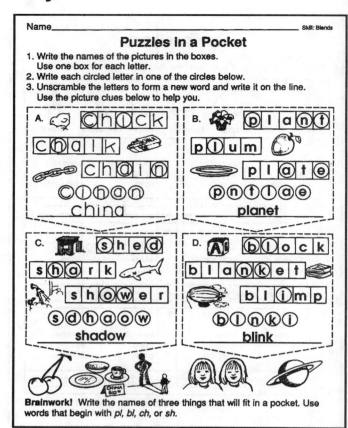

Puzzles in a Pocket

Name_____ Skill: Blends

1. Write the names of the pictures in the boxes. Use one box for each letter.
2. Write each circled letter in one of the circles below.
3. Unscramble the letters to form a new word and write it on the line. Use the picture clues below to help you.

A. Chick
chalk
chain
cinan
china

B. plant
plum
plate
pntlae
planet

C. shed
shark
shower
sdhaow
shadow

D. block
blanket
blimp
binki
blink

Brainwork! Write the names of three things that will fit in a pocket. Use words that begin with *pl, bl, ch,* or *sh.*

Page 62

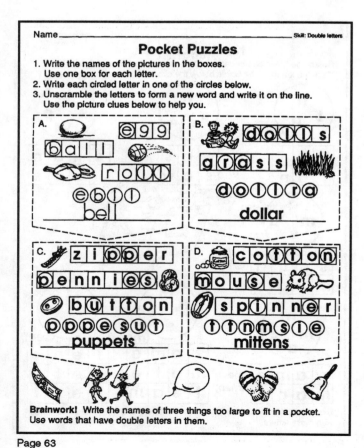

Pocket Puzzles

Name_____ Skill: Double letters

1. Write the names of the pictures in the boxes. Use one box for each letter.
2. Write each circled letter in one of the circles below.
3. Unscramble the letters to form a new word and write it on the line. Use the picture clues below to help you.

A. egg
ball
roll
ebll
bell

B. dolls
grass
dollra
dollar

C. zipper
pennies
button
pppesut
puppets

D. cotton
mouse
spinner
ttnmsie
mittens

Brainwork! Write the names of three things too large to fit in a pocket. Use words that have double letters in them.

Page 63

Pattern Pairs

Name_____ Skill: Word patterns—final e

pin   pine

Write the correct word from each pair to complete each sentence.

1. There is a __pine__ tree in the yard.   pin
2. You can hold cloth together with a __pin__.   pine
3. I need a __scrap__ of cloth.   scrap
4. I got a __scrape__ when I fell.   scrape
5. The __cute__ puppy wanted to play.   cut
6. I __cut__ the paper in half.   cute
7. The bird likes to __tap__ on the window.   tap
8. Use __tape__ to hold up the sign.   tape
9. The apple was __ripe__.   rip
10. I got a __rip__ in my new jacket.   ripe
11. We __plan__ to take a trip there.   plan
12. Grandpa came on a __plane__.   plane

Brainwork! Choose a pair of sentences above to copy and illustrate.

Page 64

120

Answer Key

Word Detective

Be a word detective. Use the clues in the Clue Box to help you decode the boldfaced words and answer the questions.

Clue Box

uni- one	tri- three
bi- two	dec- ten
cent- one hundred	

1. How many years in a **century**? one hundred

2. How many wheels on a **bicycle**? two

3. How many angles in a **triangle**? three

4. How many years in a **decade**? ten

5. How many legs on a **centipede**? one hundred

6. How many horns on a **unicorn**? one

7. How many years in a **centennial**? one hundred

8. How many wheels on a **unicycle**? one

9. How many legs on a **decapod**? ten

10. How many horns on a **triceratops**? three

Brainwork! Draw and label a unicycle, a bicycle, a tricycle. Write which you think would be the hardest to ride and why.

Page 65

Coded Tongue Twisters

Samuel Morse invented the telegraph and the Morse Code. Morse Code is a series of dots and dashes used to send messages on the telegraph.

Use the Code Box to decode the tongue twisters below.

1. Please pick

a piece of

pizza and

pass it on.

2. Susan

snacks on

sandwiches

of salty

sardines.

Morse Code Box

A	•—
B	—•••
C	—•—•
D	—••
E	•
F	••—•
G	——•
H	••••
I	••
J	•———
K	—•—
L	•—••
M	——
N	—•
O	———
P	•——•
Q	——•—
R	•—•
S	•••
T	—
U	••—
V	•••—
W	•——
X	—••—
Y	—•——
Z	——••

Brainwork! Choose a letter and use it to write a tongue twister. Write your tongue twister in Morse Code.

Page 66

Alphabet Code Puzzle

Make a code wheel by cutting out the two wheels and fastening them with a brad. Then turn the wheels so the A on the outside wheel is in line with z on the inside wheel.

A becomes z, B becomes y.

Next, complete the Reverse Code Box.

Finally, decode these names of family members.

1. nlgsvi mother
2. uzgsvi father
3. yilgsvi brother
4. hrhgvi sister
5. kvg pet
6. tizmnlgsvi grandmother
7. tizmwuzgsvi grandfather

sample

Reverse Code Box

A	z
B	y
C	x
D	w
E	v
F	u
G	t
H	s
I	r
J	q
K	p
L	o
M	n
N	m
O	l
P	k
Q	j
R	i
S	h
T	g
U	f
V	e
W	d
X	c
Y	b
Z	a

Page 67

Bag the Categories

Look carefully at the symbols used for Morse Code in the Code Box.

Fill the shopping bags with the correct letters.

Example:
Letters that are all dots
1. • E
2. •• I
3. ••• S
4. •••• H

Letters that are all dashes
1. M
2. O
3. T

Letters that start with only one dot
1. A
2. J
3. L
4. P
5. R
6. W

Letters that start with only one dash
1. B
2. C
3. D
4. K
5. N
6. X
7. Y

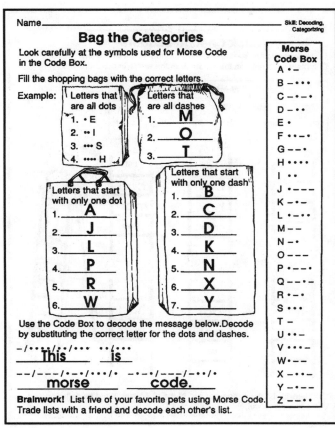

Use the Code Box to decode the message below. Decode by substituting the correct letter for the dots and dashes.

This is

morse code.

Morse Code Box

A	•—
B	—•••
C	—•—•
D	—••
E	•
F	••—•
G	——•
H	••••
I	••
J	•———
K	—•—
L	•—••
M	——
N	—•
O	———
P	•——•
Q	——•—
R	•—•
S	•••
T	—
U	••—
V	•••—
W	•——
X	—••—
Y	—•——
Z	——••

Brainwork! List five of your favorite pets using Morse Code. Trade lists with a friend and decode each other's list.

Page 68

121

Answer Key

Skill: Using a code to solve riddles

Riddles and Codes

Use the code to write the correct letter below each symbol.
You will discover the answers to some riddles.

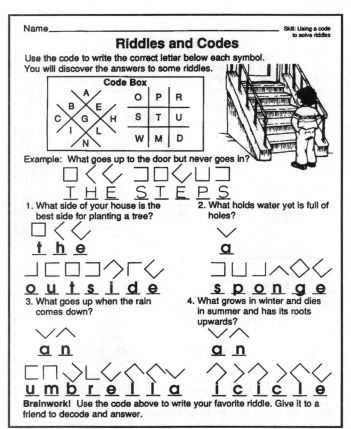

Code Box

Example: What goes up to the door but never goes in?

T H E   S T E P S

1. What side of your house is the best side for planting a tree?

t h e

o u t s i d e

2. What holds water yet is full of holes?

a

s p o n g e

3. What goes up when the rain comes down?

a n

u m b r e l l a

4. What grows in winter and dies in summer and has its roots upwards?

a n

i c i c l e

Brainwork! Use the code above to write your favorite riddle. Give it to a friend to decode and answer.

Page 69

Skill: Using a code to solve riddles

Codes and Riddles

Use the code to write the correct letter below each symbol.
You will discover the answers to some riddles.

Code Box

Example: What gets lost every time you stand up?

Y O U R   L A P

1. What is the first thing you put in a garden?

y o u r   f o o t

2. What always goes to bed with its shoes on?

a   h o r s e

3. What kind of pine has the sharpest needles?

a   p o r c u p i n e

4. What can you make that you can't use?

n o i s e

Brainwork! Use the code above to write five names.

Page 70

Skill: Letter substitution

Quick Change Ladders

Can you change **one** letter in each word to make a new word?
Complete each step on the ladder. Use the words in the Word Box.

Word Box

bay	map	tan	dot	hog
cap	ten	ban	pat	hug	cot

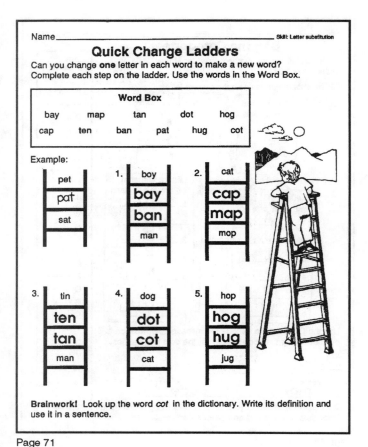

Example:

pet
pat
sat

1.
boy
bay
ban
man

2.
cat
cap
map
mop

3.
tin
ten
tan
man

4.
dog
dot
cot
cat

5.
hop
hog
hug
jug

Brainwork! Look up the word *cot* in the dictionary. Write its definition and use it in a sentence.

Page 71

Skill: Letter substitution

Quick Ladder Climb

Can you change one letter in each word to make a new word?
Complete each step on the ladder. Use the words in the Word Box.

Word Box

tell	halt	pest	poke
lean	pike	past	half
mean	tall	walk	wall

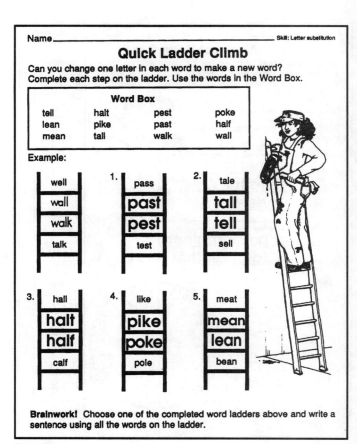

Example:

well
wall
walk
talk

1.
pass
past
pest
test

2.
tale
tall
tell
sell

3.
hall
halt
half
calf

4.
like
pike
poke
pole

5.
meat
mean
lean
bean

Brainwork! Choose one of the completed word ladders above and write a sentence using all the words on the ladder.

Page 72

Answer Key

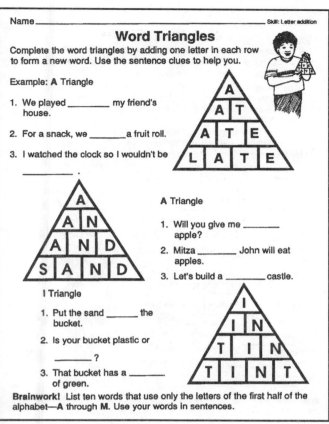

Name_____   Skill: Letter addition
Word Triangles
Complete the word triangles by adding one letter in each row to form a new word. Use the sentence clues to help you.

Example: A Triangle

1. We played _____ my friend's house.

2. For a snack, we _____ a fruit roll.

3. I watched the clock so I wouldn't be _____ .

A
A	T
A	T	E
L	A	T	E

A Triangle

1. Will you give me _____ apple?

2. Mitza _____ John will eat apples.

3. Let's build a _____ castle.

A
A	N
A	N	D
S	A	N	D

I Triangle

1. Put the sand _____ the bucket.

2. Is your bucket plastic or _____ ?

3. That bucket has a _____ of green.

I
I	N
T	I	N
T	I	N	T

Brainwork! List ten words that use only the letters of the first half of the alphabet—A through M. Use your words in sentences.

Page 73

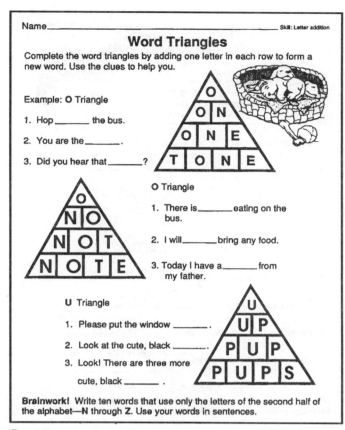

Name_____   Skill: Letter addition
Word Triangles
Complete the word triangles by adding one letter in each row to form a new word. Use the clues to help you.

Example: O Triangle

1. Hop _____ the bus.

2. You are the _____ .

3. Did you hear that _____ ?

O
O	N
O	N	E
T	O	N	E

O Triangle

1. There is _____ eating on the bus.

2. I will _____ bring any food.

3. Today I have a _____ from my father.

O
N	O
N	O	T
N	O	T	E

U Triangle

1. Please put the window _____ .

2. Look at the cute, black _____ .

3. Look! There are three more cute, black _____ .

U
U	P
P	U	P
P	U	P	S

Brainwork! Write ten words that use only the letters of the second half of the alphabet—N through Z. Use your words in sentences.

Page 74

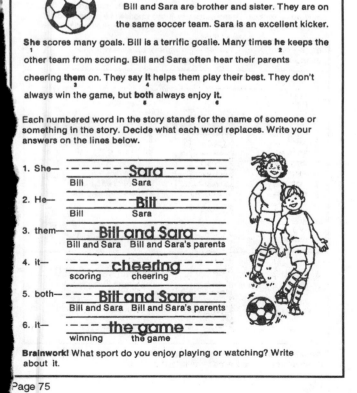

Name_____   Skill: Pronoun referents
Good Sports

Bill and Sara are brother and sister. They are on the same soccer team. Sara is an excellent kicker. **She** scores many goals. Bill is a terrific goalie. Many times **he** keeps the other team from scoring. Bill and Sara often hear their parents cheering **them** on. They say **It** helps them play their best. They don't always win the game, but **both** always enjoy **it**.

Each numbered word in the story stands for the name of someone or something in the story. Decide what each word replaces. Write your answers on the lines below.

1. She— **Sara**
   Bill / Sara

2. He— **Bill**
   Bill / Sara

3. them— **Bill and Sara**
   Bill and Sara / Bill and Sara's parents

4. it— **cheering**
   scoring / cheering

5. both— **Bill and Sara**
   Bill and Sara / Bill and Sara's parents

6. it— **the game**
   winning / the game

Brainwork! What sport do you enjoy playing or watching? Write about it.

Page 75

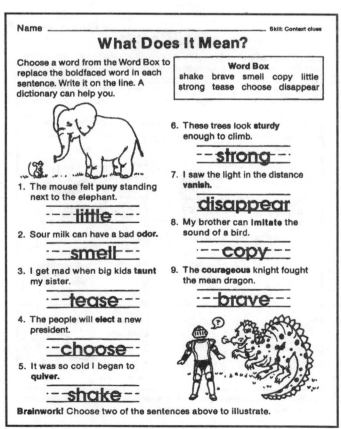

Name_____   Skill: Context clues
What Does It Mean?
Choose a word from the Word Box to replace the boldfaced word in each sentence. Write it on the line. A dictionary can help you.

Word Box
shake   brave   smell   copy   little
strong   tease   choose   disappear

1. The mouse felt **puny** standing next to the elephant.

little

2. Sour milk can have a bad **odor**.

smell

3. I get mad when big kids **taunt** my sister.

tease

4. The people will **elect** a new president.

choose

5. It was so cold I began to **quiver**.

shake

6. These trees look **sturdy** enough to climb.

strong

7. I saw the light in the distance **vanish**.

disappear

8. My brother can **imitate** the sound of a bird.

copy

9. The **courageous** knight fought the mean dragon.

brave

Brainwork! Choose two of the sentences above to illustrate.

Page 76

123

FS-32031 Reading Activities

Answer Key

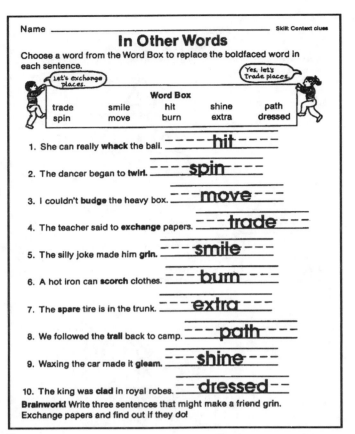

Name _____ Skill: Context clues

In Other Words

Choose a word from the Word Box to replace the boldfaced word in each sentence.

Let's exchange places.

Yes, let's Trade places.

Word Box

trade	smile	hit	shine	path
spin	move	burn	extra	dressed

1. She can really **whack** the ball. _____**hit**_____

2. The dancer began to **twirl**. _____**spin**_____

3. I couldn't **budge** the heavy box. _____**move**_____

4. The teacher said to **exchange** papers. _____**trade**_____

5. The silly joke made him **grin**. _____**smile**_____

6. A hot iron can **scorch** clothes. _____**burn**_____

7. The **spare** tire is in the trunk. _____**extra**_____

8. We followed the **trail** back to camp. _____**path**_____

9. Waxing the car made it **gleam**. _____**shine**_____

10. The king was **clad** in royal robes. _____**dressed**_____

Brainwork! Write three sentences that might make a friend grin. Exchange papers and find out if they do!

Page 77

Name _____ Skill: Context clues

Learning to Skate

Read this story about learning to skate. Then answer the questions.

Many times I had **longed** to be able to ice skate. Finally my big sister agreed to teach me.

I was filled with **glee** as I laced up my skates for the first time. I thought I would be **gliding** over the ice in minutes. Was I surprised when I stood up and fell right on the ice. It sure was **chilly**!

My sister helped me up and said, "Don't **fret**. After a few more **tumbles** you'll be skating like a star!"

1. Which boldfaced word in the story means:

   a. cold? _____**chilly**_____   d. worry? _____**fret**_____

   b. wished? _____**longed**_____   e. moving? _____**gliding**_____

   c. joy? _____**glee**_____   f. falls? _____**tumbles**_____

2. Circle the best answer.

a. The word **chilly** has to do with

   food   (temperature)   skates

b. Which would most likely fill you with **glee**?

   being sick   (a surprise party)

c. Which would you most likely **long** for?

   (a missing toy)   a broken pencil

d. When would you be most likely to **fret**?

   (if you missed the school bus)   if you got a good grade

Brainwork! Draw and label five things that can glide through the air or on the water.

Page 78

Name _____ Skill: Commonly misused words

Which Is It?

Look at each pair of words below. They look almost the same but they have different meanings. Choose the correct word for each sentence. Fill in the ○ above the word.

metal—shiny, hard material **medal**—an award	**through**—in one side and out the other **thorough**—complete	**then**—at that time **than**—a comparison

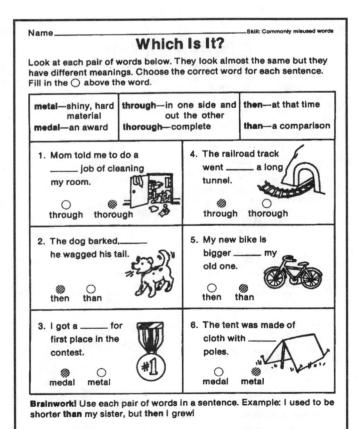

1. Mom told me to do a _____ job of cleaning my room.

   ○ through   ● thorough

2. The dog barked, _____ he wagged his tail.

   ● then   ○ than

3. I got a _____ for first place in the contest.

   ● medal   ○ metal

4. The railroad track went _____ a long tunnel.

   ● through   ○ thorough

5. My new bike is bigger _____ my old one.

   ○ then   ● than

6. The tent was made of cloth with poles.

   ○ medal   ● metal

Brainwork! Use each pair of words in a sentence. Example: I used to be shorter **than** my sister, but **then** I grew!

Page 79

Name _____ Skill: Commonly misused words

Not Quite

Some words look very much alike but have different meanings. Look at the words and their meanings below. Then choose the correct word for each sentence. Fill in the ○ above the word and write it on the line.

quite—very **quiet**—not noisy	**loose**—not tight **lose**—misplace	**guest**—visitor **guessed**—made a guess

1. We had a _____**guest**_____ for dinner.

   ● guest   ○ guessed

2. I promise not to _____**lose**_____ the note.

   ○ loose   ● lose

3. The children kept _____**quiet**_____ during the fire drill.

   ○ quite   ● quiet

4. The weather was _____**quite**_____ hot yesterday.

   ● quite   ○ quiet

5. The children _____**guessed**_____ who was behind the mask.

   ○ guest   ● guessed

6. My tooth was _____**loose**_____ so I didn't want to eat an apple.

   ○ lose   ● loose

Brainwork! "I guessed we were having a guest." Write sentences using the other two pairs of words from the Word Box.

Page 80

124

FS-32031 Reading Activities

Answer Key

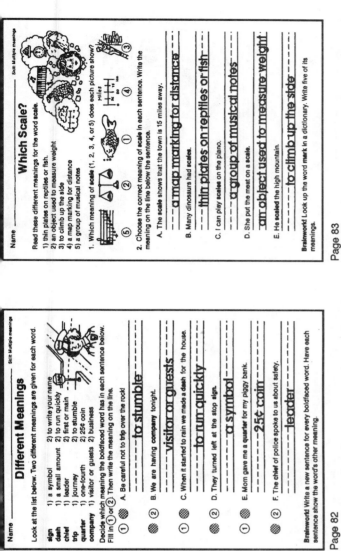

Page 83 — Which Scale?

Skill: Multiple meanings

Read these different meanings for the word **scale**.

1) thin plates on reptiles or fish
2) an object used to measure weight
3) to climb up the side
4) a map marking for distance
5) a group of musical notes

1. Which meaning of scale (1, 2, 3, 4, or 5) does each picture show?

⑤ ② ④ ① ③

2. Choose the correct meaning of **scale** in each sentence. Write the meaning on the line below the sentence.

A. The **scale** shows that the town is 15 miles away.
__a map marking for distance__

B. Many dinosaurs had **scales**.
__thin plates on reptiles or fish__

C. I can play **scales** on the piano.
__a group of musical notes__

D. She put the meat on a **scale**.
__an object used to measure weight__

E. He **scaled** the high mountain.
__to climb up the side__

Brainwork! Look up the word mark in a dictionary. Write five of its meanings.

Page 86 — Needs and Wants

Skill: Social studies vocabulary, Context

Read this story about working together. The boldfaced words may be new to you. Their meanings are given below the story. Write the word that matches each meaning.

People everywhere have the same needs. They all need food, clothing, and shelter to **survive**, or stay alive. In a community people **cooperate**, or work together, to get the things they need.
Some people provide **goods**, which are things made or grown for people to use. Other people provide **services**, or jobs that help others.
Besides needs, there are many things people want to make their lives more comfortable or fun. They buy many goods and services to enjoy in their **leisure**, or free time.

1. __cooperate__ — work together
2. __leisure__ — free time
3. __survive__ — stay alive
4. __goods__ — things made or grown for people to use
5. __services__ — jobs people do for each other

The pictures show what jobs people do. Label them **goods** or **services**.

A. __services__   B. __goods__

Brainwork! Draw and label ten pictures of goods and services you use.

Page 82 — Different Meanings

Skill: Multiple meanings

Look at the list below. Two different meanings are given for each word.

sign	1) a symbol	2) to write your name
dash	1) a small amount	2) to run quickly
chief	1) leader	2) first or main
trip	1) journey	2) to stumble
quarter	1) one-fourth	2) 25¢ coin
company	1) visitor or guests	2) business

Decide which meaning the boldfaced word has in each sentence below. Fill in ① or ②. Then write the meaning on the line.

② A. Be careful not to **trip** over the rock! __to stumble__
② B. We are having **company** tonight. __visitor or guests__
① C. When it started to rain we made a **dash** for the house. __to run quickly__
② D. They turned left at the stop **sign**. __a symbol__
① E. Mom gave me a **quarter** for my piggy bank. __25¢ coin__
② F. The **chief** of police spoke to us about safety. __leader__

Brainwork! Write a new sentence for every boldfaced word. Have each sentence show the word's other meaning.

Page 85 — Word Puzzler

Skill: Math vocabulary

Read the words in the Word Box.

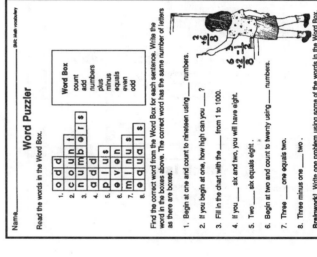

1. o d d
2. c o u n t
3. n u m b e r s
4. a d d
5. p l u s
6. e v e n
7. m i n u s
8. e q u a l s

Word Box
count
add
numbers
plus
minus
equals
even
odd

Find the correct word from the Word Box for each sentence. Write the word in the boxes above. The correct word has the same number of letters as there are boxes.

1. Begin at one and count to nineteen using ____ numbers.
2. If you begin at one, how high can you ____ ?
3. Fill in the chart with the ____ from 1 to 1000.
4. If you ____ six and two, you will have eight.
5. Two ____ six equals eight.
6. Begin at two and count to twenty using ____ numbers.
7. Three ____ one equals two.
8. Three minus one ____ two.

Brainwork! Write one problem using some of the words in the Word Box.

Page 81 — A Close Call

Look at the words and meanings below. Choose the correct word to complete each sentence. Then write the meaning of the word you chose on the line in the sentence.

desert—very dry land   **dessert**—after-meal treat

1. Dad made us pudding for a special __dessert__. __after-meal treat__
2. We drove across miles of sandy __desert__. __very dry land__

loose—miplace   **loose**—not tight

3. My brother's sweater was too __loose__. __not tight__
4. The money is in my pocket so I won't __lose__ it. __misplace__

single—only, one   **signal**—warning sign

5. The __single__ letter in the mailbox was for me. __only, one__
6. The red light was a __signal__ to stop. __warning sign__

Brainwork! What can't you do with a door? Clothes it! Write two riddles like this using the words picture and pitcher.

Page 84 — Word Puzzler

Skill: Number words

Read the words in the Word Box.

1. T h r e e
2. F o u r
3. t w o
4. s i x
5. o n e
6. S e v e n
7. f i v e
8. e i g h t

Word Box
Three
one
Four
eight
two
Seven
six
five

Find the correct word from the Word Box for each sentence. Write the word in the boxes above. The correct word has the same number of letters as there are boxes.

1. Do you know the story of The ____ Little Pigs?
2. ____ and four are eight.
3. Which one of the ____ puzzles do you want—the large one or the small one?
4. Three and three are ____.
5. Today is the baby's first birthday; she is ____ year old.
6. Do you like to play ____ Up?
7. Mom says to be home for dinner by ____ o'clock.
8. I go to bed at ____ o'clock.

Brainwork! On the back of this paper, write the number words in order from one to ten.

Answer Key

Page 89

Skill: Recognizing one-syllable words

A Single Syllable

Name _____

Remember: A word with one syllable is never divided. A word with one syllable may have one or more vowels.
Write the one-syllable word that completes the riddle.

1. What kind of fish can you find in a bird cage?
parrot   perch   tuna
perch

2. What has hands but no fingers?
kitten   clock   boat
clock

3. What has teeth but never eats?
tiger   rug   comb
comb

4. What bird is a letter of the alphabet?
robin   jay   bee
jay

5. What goes through glass without breaking it?
light   baseball   egg
light

6. What falls all the time but never gets hurt?
girl   toothbrush   snow
snow

7. What is full of holes and still holds water?
sponge   bucket   peach
sponge

8. What smells the best in a bakery?
pan   popcorn   nose
nose

Brainwork: Write a list of one-syllable words that you can make from the letters in the word friendship. List more than ten.

Page 87

Skill: Science vocabulary, Context

Looking for Energy

Name _____

Read this story about energy. The boldfaced words may be new to you. Their meanings are given below the story. Write the word that matches each meaning.

Scientists are looking for new sources, or places, to get energy. They are finding new ways to make, or produce, the power we will need in the future.
One kind of energy is geothermal. "Geo" means "earth" and "thermal" means "heat." Geothermal energy comes from heat that is already stored inside the earth.
Another kind of energy is solar. "Sol" means "sun." The sunlight is changed into energy we can use.

1. **geothermal** heat from the earth

2. **solar** from the sun

3. **produce** to make

4. **sources** places to get energy

These pictures show kinds of energy. Label them geothermal or solar.

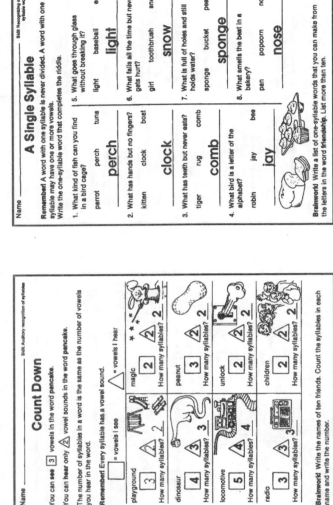

A. **solar**   B. **geothermal**

Brainwork: "-ology" means "the study of." Write what you think geology means. Then write the dictionary definition.

Page 88

Skill: Auditory recognition of syllables

Count Down

Name _____

You can see ☐ 3 vowels in the word pancake.

You can hear only △ 2 vowel sounds in the word.

The number of syllables in a word is the same as the number of vowels you hear in the word.

Remember: Every syllable has a vowel sound.
☐ = vowels I see   △ = vowels I hear

magic   △ 2   How many syllables? **2**

playground   ☐ 3 △ 2   How many syllables? **2**

peanut   △ 2   How many syllables? **2**

dinosaur   ☐ 4 △ 3   How many syllables? **3**

unlock   △ 2   How many syllables? **2**

locomotive   ☐ 5 △ 4   How many syllables? **4**

children   △ 2   How many syllables? **2**

radio   ☐ 3 △ 3   How many syllables? **3**

Brainwork: Write the names of ten friends. Count the syllables in each name and write the number.

Page 91

Skill: Suffixes as syllables

A Suffix Is a Syllable

Name _____

Remember: When a word has a suffix, the word is divided between the base word and the suffix.
Example: clear-ly

Write the word that makes sense in the sentence, dividing it into syllables. Use a hyphen.

rested   making   farmer   lumpy   sweeten
seedless   healthful   peaches   spoonful   boxes

1. Alice picked some ripe **peach-es** for Grandmother.

2. That **farm-er** grows strawberries, too.

3. These berries will **sweet-en** my cereal.

4. Dad is **mak-ing** a tasty banana bread.

5. Tracy likes **seed-less** grapes the best.

6. An orange is a **health-ful** dessert.

7. Put a **spoon-ful** of blueberries in the batter.

8. Bill likes raisins; they make his oatmeal **lump-y**.

9. I can help you put the apples in **box-es**.

10. After picking cherries, we **rest-ed**.

Brainwork: Describe yourself using four words that have suffixes.

Page 92

Skill: Prefixes and suffixes as syllables

Word Bank

Name _____

Write each word in the correct part of the piggy bank, dividing it into syllables. Use a hyphen.

windy   floating   subway   rewrite
fearless   unclear   hilly   except
inside   nonsense   kindness   painted
beaches   hopeful   rename   precook

Words With Prefixes
in-side   sub-way
un-clear   re-name
non-sense   re-write
pre-cook   ex-cept

Words With Suffixes
wind-y   hope-ful
fear-less   hill-y
beach-es   kind-ness
float-ing   paint-ed

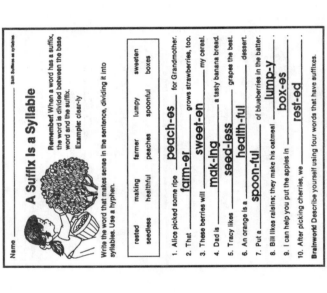

Brainwork: Make four new words from those in the Word Bank. For each new word, take off the suffix or prefix and add a new suffix or prefix.

Page 90

Skill: Prefixes as syllables

Prefixes Are Syllables

Name _____

Remember: When a word has a prefix, the word is divided between the prefix and the base word.
Example: re-turn

Circle the word that has a prefix. Write the word, using a hyphen to divide it into syllables.

1. My little sister is in (preschool). **pre-school**

2. Mom (unlocked) the garage door. **un-locked**

3. Grandpa watched the (replay). **re-play**

4. Aunt Susan will (unwrap) the box. **un-wrap**

5. My brother (reset) the clock. **re-set**

6. Dad drinks (nonfat) milk. **non-fat**

7. The twins look (alike). **a-like**

8. I like to ride the (subway). **sub-way**

9. Uncle Joe can (explain) his math. **ex-plain**

10. Grandma will (repaint) my bike. **re-paint**

11. My cousin went (indoors). **in-doors**

12. Theresa likes to (explore). **ex-plore**

Brainwork: List at least six words that have the prefix un.

Working With Syllables

Write the word that makes sense in the sentence, dividing it into syllables. Use a hyphen.

| doctor | sister | suppose |
| hungry | children | thirteen |

1. Our class has twenty-six __chil-dren__.
2. Where do you __sup-pose__ Kelly is?
3. Dan read __thir-teen__ books last summer.
4. Are you getting __hun-gry__ for lunch?
5. Jenny is my older __sis-ter__.
6. The __doc-tor__ gave Mother some medicine.

Check your work. Write each word divided into syllables on the blanks below. Be sure to use a blank for the hyphen, too.
Check: Is every hyphen in the box?

1. c h i l - d r e n
2. s u p - p o s e
3. t h i r - t e e n
4. h u n - g r y
5. s i s - t e r
6. d o c - t o r

Brainworld Find the answer words that have three vowels. Write a sentence for each one.

Page 95

What's the Rule?

Rule A: When one consonant comes between two vowels in a word, and the first vowel is short, the word is usually divided after the consonant. Example: riv-er

Rule B: When one consonant comes between two vowels in a word, and the first vowel is long, the word is usually divided before the consonant. Example: tu-ture

Read each word. Write A or B for the rule that tells how to divide it. Then write the word, dividing it into syllables. Use a hyphen.

1. music __B__ __mu-sic__   7. spider __B__ __spi-der__
2. seven __A__ __sev-en__   8. river __A__ __riv-er__
3. robin __A__ __rob-in__   9. baby __B__ __ba-by__
4. bacon __B__ __ba-con__   10. salad __A__ __sal-ad__
5. paper __B__ __pa-per__   11. china __B__ __chi-na__
6. second __A__ __sec-ond__   12. silent __B__ __si-lent__

Brainworld Choose three words from above. Write a sentence for each one.

Page 98

Syllable Fun

Remember! When three consonants come between two vowels in a word, the word is usually divided between the first two consonants.
Example: sur-prise

Write the word from the Word Box that makes sense in the sentence.

Word Box: surprise, hungry, hundred, Pilgrims, children

1. His great grandmother lived to be a __hundred__ years old.
2. The playground was full of noisy __children__.
3. The singing telegram was a big __surprise__.
4. At Thanksgiving I read about the __Pilgrims__.
5. Before breakfast Sue is very __hungry__.

Write the answer words from the sentences above, dividing them into syllables. Use a hyphen.
1. __hun-dred__   3. __sur-prise__
2. __chil-dren__   4. __Pil-grims__
5. __hun-gry__

Brainworld Make a list of ten breakfast foods. Write the number of syllables beside each word.

Page 94

Choose a Word

Remember! When one consonant comes between two vowels in a word, and the first vowel is long, the word is usually divided before the consonant.
Example: tō-fa

Write the word that names each picture. Use a hyphen to divide it into syllables. Mark ⎺ over the first vowel if it is long.

1. tī-ger
2. pā-per
3. mū-sic
4. rō-bot
5. spī-der
6. bā-by
7. bā-con
8. pū-pil
9. pī-rate
10. tū-ba

tiger, baby, pirate, robot, paper, tuba, music, bacon, pupil, spider

Brainworld Choose three words from the word list. Write a sentence for each one.

Page 97

Syllable Study

Remember! When two consonants come between two vowels in a word, the word is usually divided between the two consonants.

Example: sis-ver

Write each word, dividing it into syllables. Use a hyphen. If a word cannot be divided, circle it.

1. window __win-dow__   11. garden __gar-den__
2. lesson __les-son__   12. monkey __mon-key__
3. butter __but-ter__   13. walnut __wal-nut__
4. (broom)   14. picnic __pic-nic__
5. parrot __par-rot__   15. winter __win-ter__
6. picture __pic-ture__   16. (might)
7. almost __al-most__   17. suppose __sup-pose__
8. number __num-ber__   18. doctor __doc-tor__
9. happen __hap-pen__   19. thirteen __thir-teen__
10. (dark)   20. sister __sis-ter__

Brainworld Make a list of all the vowels and another list of all the consonants.

Page 93

More Syllables

Remember! When one consonant comes between two vowels in a word, and the first vowel is short, the word is usually divided after the consonant.
Example: rĭv-er

Read each sentence. Look at the word in bold type. Mark ˘ over the first short vowel. Write the word, dividing it into syllables. Use a hyphen.

1. Did you see a **robin** in the nest? __rŏb-in__
2. Brad is a good figure skater. __fĭg-ure__
3. I had some melon for lunch. __mĕl-on__
4. Her pet lizard escaped. __lĭz-ard__
5. Put the groceries in the wagon. __wăg-on__
6. The lemon tree is blossoming. __lĕm-on__
7. Abe grew up in a log cabin. __căb-in__
8. My shadow looks ten feet tall. __shăd-ow__
9. Where are the seven new books? __sĕv-en__
10. Look at the planet Mars. __plăn-et__

Brainworld On the back of this paper, write two of the above sentences. Then write the number of syllables above each word in the sentence.

Page 96

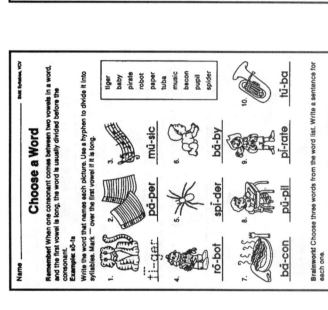
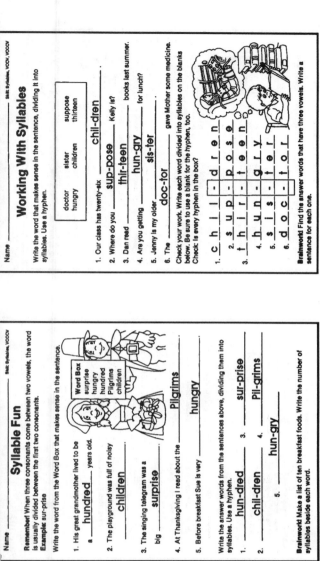

Answer Key

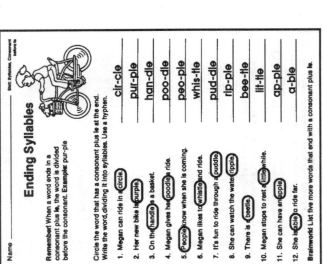

Name

Skill: Syllables; Consonant before le

Ending Syllables

Remember: When a word ends in a consonant plus **le**, the word is divided before the consonant. Example: pur-ple

Circle the word that has a consonant plus **le** at the end. Write the word, dividing it into syllables. Use a hyphen.

1. Megan can ride in (circle)   cir-cle
2. Her new bike is (purple)   pur-ple
3. On the (handle) a basket.   han-dle
4. Megan gives her (poodle) ride.   poo-dle
5. (People) know when she is coming.   peo-ple
6. Megan likes to (whistle) and ride.   whis-tle
7. It's fun to ride through (puddle)   pud-dle
8. She can watch the water (ripple)   rip-ple
9. There is a (beetle)   bee-tle
10. Megan stops to rest a (little) while.   lit-tle
11. She can have an (apple)   ap-ple
12. She is (able) to ride far.   a-ble

Brainwork: List five more words that end with a consonant plus **le**.

Page 101

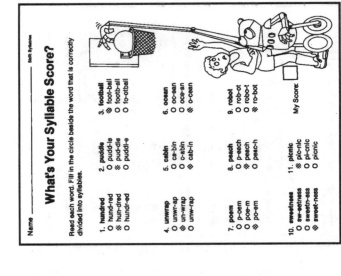

Name

Skill: Syllables

What's Your Syllable Score?

Read each word. Fill in the circle beside the word that is correctly divided into syllables.

1. **hundred**
   ○ hund-red
   ⊗ hun-dred
   ○ hundr-ed

2. **puddle**
   ○ pud-le
   ⊗ pud-dle
   ○ puddl-e

3. **football**
   ⊗ foot-ball
   ○ footb-all
   ○ fo-otball

4. **unwrap**
   ○ unwr-ap
   ⊗ un-wrap
   ○ unw-rap

5. **cabin**
   ○ ca-bin
   ○ c-abin
   ⊗ cab-in

6. **ocean**
   ○ oc-ean
   ○ oce-an
   ⊗ o-cean

7. **poem**
   ○ p-oem
   ○ poe-m
   ⊗ po-em

8. **peach**
   ○ p-each
   ⊗ peach
   ○ peac-h

9. **robot**
   ○ rob-ot
   ○ robo-t
   ⊗ ro-bot

10. **sweetness**
    ○ sw-eetness
    ○ sweetn-ess
    ⊗ sweet-ness

11. **picnic**
    ⊗ pic-nic
    ○ p-icnic
    ○ picnic

My Score: _____

Page 104

Name

Skill: Syllables; Two vowels sounded separately

Thinking About Syllables

Remember: When two vowels are together in a word and have separate sounds, the word is divided between the two vowels.

Example: li-on

Write the word below that makes sense in the sentence. Use hyphens to divide the word into syllables.

| poem | poet | cruel | giant | diet |
| science | radio | create | lion | idea |

1. Someone who writes a poem is a _____   po-et
2. Todd has written a _____   po-em
3. It's about a huge _____   gi-ant
4. The giant had a pet _____   li-on
5. He was kind, not _____   cru-el
6. The giant shrank when he went on a _____   di-et
7. Where did Todd get the _____ to write?   i-de-a
8. He listened to the _____   ra-di-o
9. It was fun to _____   cre-ate   a giant.
10. Todd likes writing and _____   sci-ence   , too.

Brainwork: Write a poem about something you learned in science.

Page 100

Name

Skill: Syllables

I Know Syllables!

Read each rule. Then write the words, dividing them into syllables.

1. When one consonant comes between two vowels in a word, and the first vowel is short, the word is usually divided after the consonant.
   second   sec-ond
   river   riv-er

2. When one consonant comes between two vowels in a word, and the first vowel is long, the word is usually divided before the consonant.
   spider   spi-der
   future   fu-ture

3. When a vowel is sounded alone in a word, it is a syllable by itself.
   erase   e-rase
   open   o-pen

4. When two vowels are together in a word and have separate sounds, the word is divided between the two vowels.
   poet   po-et
   lion   li-on

5. When a word ends in a consonant plus **le**, the word is divided before the consonant.
   purple   pur-ple
   little   lit-tle

Brainwork: Choose one of the rules above. Write five words that follow that rule.

Page 103

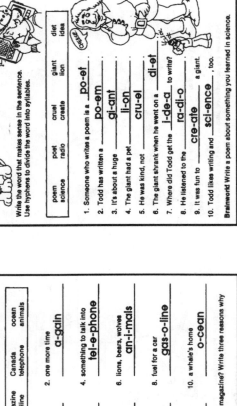

Name

Skill: Syllables; Vowel sounded alone

Word Choice

Remember: When a vowel is sounded alone in a word, it is a syllable by itself.
Examples: e-rase, dis-a-gree

Write each word below its definition, dividing it into syllables.

| again | open | magazine | Canada | ocean |
| Irish | alive | gasoline | telephone | animals |

1. not closed   o-pen
2. one more time   a-gain
3. from Ireland   I-rish
4. something to talk into   tel-e-phone
5. something to read   mag-a-zine
6. lions, bears, wolves   an-i-mals
7. a country   Can-a-da
8. fuel for a car   gas-o-line
9. living   a-live
10. a whale's home   o-cean

Brainwork: What is your favorite magazine? Write three reasons why it's your favorite.

Page 99

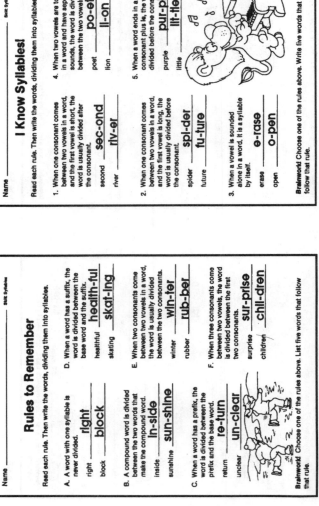

Name

Skill: Syllables

Rules to Remember

Read each rule. Then write the words, dividing them into syllables.

A. A word with one syllable is never divided.
   right   right
   block   block

B. A compound word is divided between the two words that make the compound word.
   inside   in-side
   sunshine   sun-shine

C. When a word has a prefix, the word is divided between the prefix and the base word.
   return   re-turn
   unclear   un-clear

D. When a word has a suffix, the word is divided between the base word and the suffix.
   healthful   health-ful
   skating   skat-ing

E. When two consonants come between two vowels in a word, the word is usually divided between the two consonants.
   winter   win-ter
   rubber   rub-ber

F. When three consonants come between two vowels, the word is divided between the first two consonants.
   surprise   sur-prise
   children   chil-dren

Brainwork: Choose one of the rules above. List five words that follow that rule.

Page 102

FS-32031 Reading Activities